Best wishes,

Roger Evans

THE BOOK OF

BRIDGWATER

Medieval Markets to Modern-Day Carnivals

ROGER EVANS

HALSGROVE

First published in Great Britain in 2006

British Library Cataloguing-in-Publication Data
A CIP record for this title is available from the British Library

ISBN 1 84114 509 2
ISBN 978 1 84114 509 9

HALSGROVE

Halsgrove House
Lower Moor Way
Tiverton, Devon EX16 6SS
Tel: 01884 243242
Fax: 01884 243325
Email: sales@halsgrove.com
Website: www.halsgrove.com

Frontispiece photograph: *St Mary's Church, 1905.* (Courtesy Douglas Allen)

Printed and bound in Great Britain by CPI Bath

CONTENTS

Introduction

In 1995 I published the story of my home town of Bridgwater in the book *Bridgwater With and Without the E*. The 'with' referred to the 17 other Bridgewaters around the world which are spelt with the 'e' included. The book sold out three times, demonstrating the enthusiasm within the town for local history. It was time for a relaunch but, by then, more information about Bridgwater had become available and I knew the time was right for a completely new volume. Perhaps the most important of the new contributions were the enlightening recreations of Bridgwater Castle by artist Michael Stirling. Never before had we an idea of how the castle would have looked in its heyday. I am grateful to Michael for his permission to reproduce those images here.

In addition, further archaeological evidence has become available and we generally know more about the history of our town. Here I acknowledge the invaluable input of Chris Sidaway, who has such an in-depth knowledge of the medieval period of Bridgwater's history, and who worked with Michael Stirling and myself on the recreation of the castle.

Another significant change came a few years ago when I purchased, at auction, a photographic collection which I believe to be predominantly the work of Robert Gillo, who painstakingly recorded images of the town around 1865 and was resident at 32 Friarn Street at the time. It was my intention to prevent such a valuable collection of prints and original glass-plate negatives from leaving the town. Thanks to the Bridgwater Charter Trustees, and now the Bridgwater Town Council, that collection is in the safe keeping of the Blake Museum, and I am grateful to their staff for scanning many of the images shown in this publication.

This volume focuses on my home town of Bridgwater, from Celts to carnival, from Saxons to suburbia, covering the town's history and character.

In 1841, the Bristol-based makers of this milestone proved their inability to spell...
(FROM THE ROGER EVANS COLLECTION)

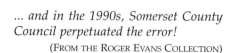

... and in the 1990s, Somerset County Council perpetuated the error!
(FROM THE ROGER EVANS COLLECTION)

CHAPTER 1

The Dark Ages – Winding Back the Clock

Imagine that you are floating high over Bridgwater and that you have been gifted with the power to observe as time goes in reverse. As you watch, the boundaries of the town shrink back towards the centre, estates of thousands of homes revert to green fields. The motorway disappears, two road bridges over the river disappear, along with Broadway. Summer traffic is queued back for miles either side of the Town Bridge. Quantock Road vanishes, closely followed by Bristol Road.

Pines Garage on Taunton Road, c.1910, demolished in the 1950s when Broadway was constructed. (COURTESY MURRAY STEWART)

The clock reverses even faster and all roads and railway lines fade away, replaced by muddy tracks. People, but not very many, are travelling around on foot or on horseback.

A solitary bridge crosses the river and, in the blink of an eye, as the clock continues its backward run, the iron bridge disappears and alongside where once it stood is a stone-built bridge, defended by a huge castle. Medieval ships are sailing up the river and mooring outside the castle whilst barges wait on the other side of the bridge to take goods deeper into Somerset. Although small, it's a bustling little town with no more than a dozen streets, mostly on the castle side of the river where the spireless church stands.

In another blink of an eye, the bridge and castle have gone, the bustle of the town has disappeared, just a few simple houses lie scattered around, on the higher ground at Hamp, Durleigh and Wembdon. And there, where we are used to seeing St Mary's Church, is a little timber and thatched Saxon church.

We stop the clock and look at the time. It's AD1065. William the Conqueror has yet to reach our shores. It's 600 years since the Romans went home and for 600 years, this area alongside the River Parrett has experienced the Dark Ages. But nothing ever happens here.

It's not that kind of place. Down at Combwich there was a battle between the Anglo-Saxons and the Danes, and the Celts and the Anglo-Saxons have been clashing all over the place. The Romans once had forts over at Puriton and at Cannington. More recently, though, King Alfred passed by a couple of times but didn't stop. There was no reason. Nothing ever happened in Bridgwater – but that was all to change.

Bryj!

We're still stuck back in AD1065 and Bridgwater is an insignificant little place without even a bridge across the river. Ships sailing up the River Parrett simply pass by, just the occasional one mooring at the quayside, perhaps to unload goods but likely just waiting for the next tide to continue their journey upstream. The place is not even called Bridgwater; it is simply called 'The Quayside', but it is called that in Anglo-Saxon – 'Bryj'. Folks have lived here for generations, mostly on the west side of the river, on the higher ground. The other side is pretty well impassable, other than during the summer months when there are trackways which can be followed up to the Polden Hills. But on the west side of the river, up at Hamp, at some time in the future, a stone axe will be discovered, a Bronze Age urn will be found in Colley Lane, and archaeologists will reveal that trackways once led down from Wembdon Hill and Durleigh to the River Parrett at Crowpill, where a Roman coin will also be discovered, along with Anglo-Saxon pottery in King Square. All these items will provide evidence of a settlement dating back at least 1,000 years.

But those glory days have yet to come.

❖

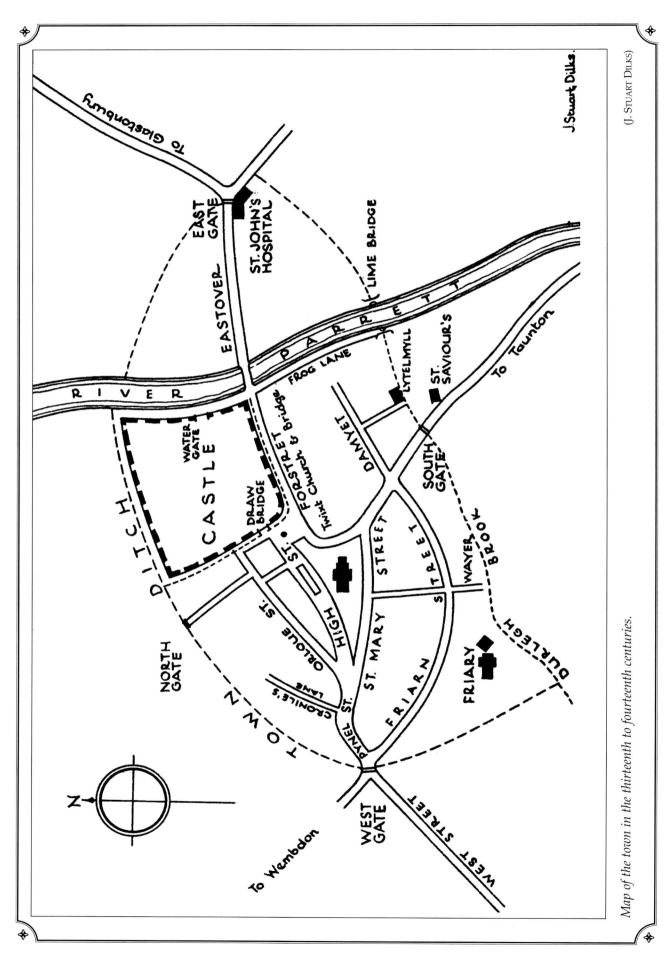

J. Stuart Dilks.

(J. STUART DILKS)

Map of the town in the thirteenth to fourteenth centuries.

CHAPTER 2

The Middle Ages – 1066 and All That

Prior to the arrival of William the Conqueror in 1066, Harold was on the throne and Bridgwater, still called just Bryj, was just one of many communities which came under the lordship of the Saxon Merleswain. Merleswain was not even a local man. As the Sheriff of Lincolnshire and a close friend of the king, Bridgwater was in his lordship and in the North Petherton hundred. In other words, Bridgwater was not the centre of the local universe, North Petherton was. The size of Bridgwater relative to its neighbours can be gathered from the danegeld collected. Around AD998, Ethelred II, then king, came to a financial arrangement with the Danes. In what was a protection racket, he paid them £66,000 and they promised not to cause any trouble. Ethelred then imposed taxes on communities across the country in order to get his money back. The taxes imposed locally were as follows:

Middlezoy	*12 shillings*
Bridgwater	*5 shillings*
Puriton	*5 shillings*
Stogursey	*4 shillings and 6 pence*
Woolavington	*4 shillings*
Wembdon	*3 shillings*
Durleigh	*6 pence*

So we can see that Bridgwater had no more significance than many of the villages in the area and had yet to find its place in history. William the Conqueror helped it on its way. In 1066 William invaded England and gave parcels of land to his supporters as a thank-you gift. Bridgwater, Wembdon, Bawdrip, Horsey, Pawlett, Huntspill, Burnham and Brean, along with various other manors, were given to Walter, from Douai in France. Walter, however, took up residence in Bampton in Devon, but Bryj, the quayside on the River Parrett, now belonged to him and from that time became known as Walter's Quayside, Bryj of Walter, Bridgwater.

Though the Saxons had had their day, Saxon names survived. Sydenham was Saxon for wide meadow, Hamp was a homestead, Bryg was a quayside or, some believe, a fording place, and the town was split into Eastover and Westover, in fact 'estufer' and 'westufer', 'ufer' being Saxon for bank, hence east and west bank. But there was still no bridge!

Between 1080 and 1086, at the request of the king, an inventory was taken across the nation and recorded in what became known as the Domesday Book. The entry for Bridgwater contains the following, (in Latin):

Walter holds Brugie. Merleswain held it at the time of King Edward, and it was assessed at the Dane-Geld for 5 hides. The arable land is 10 carucates. In demesne [the land held by the Lord himself] are 3 carucates and 5 servants, 13 villanes [slaves], 9 bordars [wood cutters and the like] and 5 cottagers with 8 ploughs. There is a mill of 5 shillings rent and 10 acres of meadow, and 100 acres of coppiced wood and 30 acres of pasture. When Walter received it, it was worth 100 shillings [£5] and is now worth £7.

A hide is basically an extended family and the land which supports it, while a carucate can be equated to the amount of land an ox is capable of ploughing. So we have a picture of a small community of perhaps five extended families with, nearby, Sydenham, a quarter of a hide held by Roger of Arundel (previously held by a Saxon called Chepping), and Hamp, with its one hide, four ploughs, four slaves, one villager, seven smallholders with one plough, 15 acres of meadow and three acres of woodland. Each of these was a separate community. Then, on each side of the town, there appeared to be the farms which gave us East Bower and West Bower, the latter on the edge of Durleigh. Just beyond Sydenham, completing the picture of these small farming homesteads, was Horsey, capable of supporting seven teams of plough, almost twice as many as Hamp. Nearby North Petherton was three times the size of Bridgwater.

It appears that Walter did little to improve or develop the town. In time the estate passed to his son, Robert of Bampton, and then to Robert's daughter, Gillian. By this time she owned several other estates and, on her marriage, they all passed to Fulke Pagnell (the family whose name survives in Penel Orlieu). Their son ran up some heavy debts and fell out of favour with the king – in fact at one time he had to flee the country. To sort out his finances and regain royal favour, in 1199, he passed his estates to William Brewer, a close confidant of the king. Brewer was trusted by four kings of England: Henry II, Richard I, John and Henry III. That trust worked to Bridgwater's benefit.

William Brewer

The turning point for Bridgwater came in the year 1200, when King John was on the throne. In earlier years, Brewer had been instrumental in delivering the ransom money which paid for the release of

Scenes from the Bridgwater Pageant of 1927 depicting King John granting the charter.

(FROM THE ROGER EVANS COLLECTION)

Richard the Lionheart from incarceration in Germany. In 1215 he would be at King John's side, advising on the signing of the Magna Carta. Brewer recognised the potential for Bridgwater to be more than just a quayside. He knew that, if a bridge could be thrown across the river, the village would become a strategic point in Somerset, the tall-masted ships bringing goods in from the Bristol Channel being unable to sail beyond the bridge. Thus Bridgwater would become a transport depot, where sea-borne goods would be transferred from ships to barges, and horse and foot traffic would cross the River Parrett using the new bridge, unhindered by the tide.

Such a crossroads of road and river would require a castle to defend it. King John, in his second year on the throne, was with William Brewer in France, travelling to Chinon, near Tours. On the way, Brewer suggested to King John that Bridgwater was an ideal location for a bridge and a castle. As the day progressed, scribes began to draw up the charter which would grant Bridgwater its freedom, giving it borough status, allowing burgage rent to be collected by the town's reeves and putting an end to serfdom. During the evening of 26 June 1200, King John placed his seal upon the charter and Bridgwater, as a free town, was born. It was time for William Brewer to turn his vision into reality. A town with a bridge, a commercial centre unlike any other in the county.

The Charter Translated

John, by the Grace of God, et cetera. Know ye that we have given and granted, and have confirmed, by this present charter, to our beloved and faithful William Brewer, that Bridgwater shall be a free borough and that there be a free market there, and a fair every year that shall last during eight days, that is to say, from the day of the nativity of the Blessed John the Baptist; with paagio *[tolls for pasturage],* pontage *[tolls for using the bridge],* passage *[ferry money],* lastage *[tolls for loading and unloading vessels],* stallage *[for stalls at the fair or market], with all the other liberties and free customs appertaining to a free borough, and to a market and fair. We grant also to the aforesaid William that the aforesaid burgesses of the aforesaid borough be free burgesses, and be quit of all toll, pontage, passage, lastage and stallage, and have all liberties and free customs and quittances which appertain to us through our land, except the City of London. Wherefore we will and firmly ordain that the aforesaid William, and his heirs after him, have and hold all the things aforesaid well and in peace, happily and quietly, wholly and fully, and honourably, with all their liberties and free customs as aforesaid.*

The document was witnessed by the Earls of Pembroke, Chester, Salisbury and others. There were, in fact, three charters, one granting permission to build a castle, another permitting the free borough and a third permitting various fairs and markets. The freedom of the burgages was a significant benefit to the townsfolk. Until the granting of the charter, anyone who worked the land was obliged to give occasional days of service to the lord of the manor. Inevitably this obligation would be called on at the very time the individual was busiest, perhaps at harvest time. The end of serfdom meant that an individual could pay a tax instead, probably about a day's pay. The going rate was a shilling per burgage per year and the penalty for non-payment was to have one's doors sealed up until settlement was made.

The burgesses, that privileged band of people who had their own businesses, were allowed to hold their own court once a month on a Monday to deal with minor crimes; trespass, fraud, debt and environmental issues such as ditch clearance, the removal of offal, short measure, trading too close to someone selling the same items and regrating. This latter offence is committed when an item is bought and then sold at a higher price on the same day. Punishments included imprisonment, pillory and tumbrel or cucking-stool. With the pillory, the offender would be placed in stocks with hands and head fixed in place. Townsfolk could then throw obnoxious matter at the offenders. The tumbrel was a wooden stump on which the offender had to sit and receive similar punishment. One Bridgwater offender to suffer in the pillory was a lady who had failed to re-site a dung heap which was close to her cottage in the town. Pillories and stocks were in use as recently as 1782, when they were sited at the Cornhill having spent 40 years outside the Town Hall. Ancient stocks can still be found under the yew tree in Wembdon churchyard.

In the years that followed, Brewer entertained King John at Bridgwater on at least five occasions; 4 and 15 July 1204; 1 and 2 September 1205; 19 September 1208 and 22 September 1210. In 1245, John's son, Henry III, stayed in the town. Almost certainly, King John's interest was primarily in the excellent hunting to be had in Somerset which, for that very reason, was his favourite county. From the pipe rolls of the Bishop of Winchester, we learn that payments were made for salting and drying venison from Bridgwater, reflecting the abundance of deer.

Under Brewer's guardianship, the town began to prosper. He built the bridge, originally a wooden affair, and between 1200 and 1210 he built the castle, a magnificent structure, to defend the bridge and the town.

Bridgwater Castle

Bridgwater Castle was an impressive building for its day, covering 10 acres and big enough to support 2,000–3,000 troops in times of strife. It had walls 12–15ft thick and was surrounded on three sides by a 30ft moat, on the fourth side being the river. The north moat was known as the Common Ditch and the other two sides as the Castle Ditch. The boundaries, as we would recognise them today, would be the river on the west, Fore Street on the south, Chandos Street to the north and Castle Moat to the west. Within this area the castle was split into the upper bailey (roughly King Square and all the surrounding buildings) and the lower bailey, being everything between King Square and the river. Stand at the top of Castle Street today and you can see how the upper bailey was on level ground and the lower bailey was on the bank sloping down to the river.

The layout is well illustrated in the reproductions used here. The author is indebted to Chris Sidaway for the archaeological input and to Michael Stirling for the actual reproduction. Thanks to their efforts, we now have a reasonable idea of how the castle would have looked in its heyday. The upper and lower baileys were divided by a defensive wall. Part of this divide was taken up by the keep. Should the castle come under attack from the river or the Cornhill direction, then the defenders within could retreat back into a smaller but more defendable area. There were two main entrances into the castle, the Watergate from the river and the Market Gate leading into the market place at the Cornhill, where York Buildings stand today. Each of these entrances was protected by barbican towers plus a drawbridge

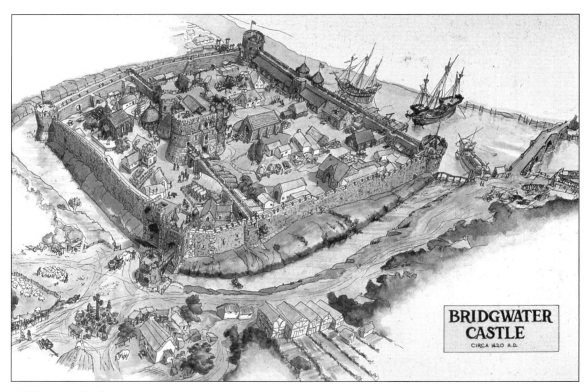

Bridgwater Castle.   (Courtesy Michael Stirling)

and portcullis. Evidence of the outer walls can still be found at the Watergate Restaurant on the West Quay, where the Romanesque arch is still clearly visible; at the private car parking area at the bottom of Chandos Street, where a large section of wall is clearly visible; and at the back of Boots the Chemist, where a section of wall and evidence of a well can be seen. The walls were built mainly of red Wembdon sandstone, on a foundation of Blue Lias from central Somerset. Archways and windows were trimmed with the fawn-coloured Ham stone from South Somerset.

Within the castle walls there was St Mark's Chapel (looked after by the brethren of St John's), stables, a smithy, an armoury to serve the troops, a bell tower and a dovecote which provided fertiliser for the vegetable gardens. Many of these buildings were roofed with green-glazed tiles, the source of which remains unknown. Within Mortimer's Hall, being the great hall within the keep, there was a raised dais where the privileged would sit. Vaults below ground level acted as both dungeons and wine cellars. There are numerous buildings in the Castle Street area where these undercroft vaults still exist and some were used by the Customs House which, once at the lower end of Castle Street, accounts for the naming of Bond Street.

By the mid-1300s it appears the castle was falling into disrepair. The moats were overgrown with reeds, which provided useful thatching material, and houses were springing up inside the walls. Despite this decline, the castle served a military purpose for many years to come.

The Execution of Humphrey Stafford

Within the walls were the various apparatuses of punishment. Stocks, pillories, cucking-stool and apparatus for executions. One example of the ultimate punishment was the execution of Humphrey Stafford, the Earl of Devon, who had displeased the king. Stafford was the constable of Bristol and Bridgwater Castle. As a Privy Councillor he was sent by Edward IV to join forces with the Earl of Pembrokeshire in an assault on the Yorkshire rebel known as Robin of Redesdale. Stafford travelled to Banbury with his 600 bowmen. It appears that the night before they were due to attack the rebel forces, Humphrey Stafford and the Earl of Pembroke fell out as the result of an argument. Legend has it that it was over the favours of a 'faire damsel' at the inn where they were staying. Stafford lost the toss and, in a huff, withdrew his troops and went home. The following day, when battle commenced without Stafford's bowmen, the Earl of Pembroke lost 5,000 Welshmen, slain by the men from the north. The king, furious with Stafford's behaviour, declared that the Sheriffs of Devon and Somerset were to 'make diligent search for Humphrey Stafford, Earl of Devon, and execute him without delay.' On his way to Bridgwater Castle at the time, he was captured at Brent Marsh, near Brent Knoll. He was taken to Bridgwater Castle and there, on 17 August 1470, he was beheaded.

Was Humphrey Stafford the only execution within the castle? Almost certainly not. When the foundations were being built for the sheltered

Bridgwater Castle.

(Courtesy Michael Stirling)

accommodation now known as Home Castle House, in Chandos Street, a number of skeletons were found. Strangely, the heads were separate from the bodies. The bones were gathered together and re-interred in Wembdon churchyard. It is known that apart from the two main entrances to the castle, i.e. the Watergate and the Market Gate, there was also an exit in the north-east corner of the castle through which were taken the bodies of the executed. Perhaps the idea was that they be washed away by the river. Perhaps some remained buried in the silt of the moat.

Control of the Castle

On the death of William Brewer, the control of the castle passed to his son, also William, who was the last of the male line. On his death, his estates were divided between his five sisters and the castle, with the manor and town of Bridgwater, passed to the eldest, Graecia, who had married William de Broase, a Welsh baron. In 1233 Graecia's son and heir, William, was killed by Llewellyn, Prince of Wales and the eldest of that William's four daughters, Maud, inherited the estate. She had married into the Mortimer family, the most powerful family in Wales, and hence it was there that the family spent their time. As a consequence, Bridgwater Castle, in the absence of the owner, was governed by an appointed constable. Generations of Mortimers

owned the castle until, in 1424, Anne Mortimer married Richard, Earl of Pembroke, and the castle became the property of the Crown. Meanwhile, the town grew within its own boundaries and, outside, grew another community, that of Haygrove. Hence numerous medieval documents refer to 'Bridgwater including Haygrove'. In total Bridgwater, in the mid-1250s, included 115 acres of farm, 140 acres of various cereals, two ploughmen, a carter and 19 tenant farmers. Around the town were a number of arable fields, Blacklands at Crowpill, Northfields, St Matthew's Field and Hay Field, the latter probably at Haygrove. Each of these survives today in place names and each in turn pre-dates the formation of the town itself.

In 1485, the Crown granted the estate to Giles, Lord Daubeney, who was succeeded by his son, Henry, in 1508. But it was not enough for Henry, who wanted the title of 'Earl of Bridgwater'. In his endeavours to acquire the title, he spent most of his fortune and was obliged to sell the estate to Edward Seymour, the owner of West Bower.

Governance of the Town

During the medieval years, the town was governed by the burgesses, who formed themselves into the Guild of Merchants. Amongst their many privileges was their entitlement to have the first option on purchasing any new goods brought to the town during the first three weeks of their availability. Members of the guild and local taxpayers were allowed to trade without toll within the town. Others paid a toll to the guild. Membership of the guild also permitted the member to trade anywhere in the country without toll except in London. It is easy to see how powerful the guild members became. Apart from them, it was perhaps the church which was the next most influential body within the town. This situation was maintained until 18 June 1468, when a new charter relaxed the rules. The following year, Bridgwater elected its first mayor, John Kendall, and two bailiffs, replacing the previous system of reeves. Although the system for governance had changed, the power base remained with the same individuals. The governance of the borough under the chairmanship of the mayor, with aldermen elected for life from within their own ranks, was a system which remained in place until local government reorganisation in 1974.

John Kendall was clearly a man of great influence. Not only was he the town's first mayor but at the time he was the town's representative in Parliament and undoubtedly would have had considerable input into the terms of the new charter. Kendall was a trader in cloth, the commodity upon which the town's wealth was based.

Criminal Justice

Through the thirteenth century, a court represented the borough and Haygrove. The lord of the manor had a gallows, tumbrel and pillories and a right to wrecks of the sea. During the fourteenth century there were three systems of courts within the castle. First there was the borough court, which met monthly and appointed two each of reeves, bailiffs ale-tasters and bread-weighers, a single janitor to attend the town gates and a group of wardens who kept an eye on the dozen or so streets in the town. They could impose fines for offences and, if the miscreant was unable to pay in cash, the court could demand possession of goods to the value of the fine, typically anything from a brass pot to a horse. Beyond fines came the tumbrel or cucking-stool or, worse still, the pillory.

The second court was the Piepowder court, which survived from 1378 right through to the eighteenth century, the records of 1735 showing seven men failing to pay their tolls at St Matthew's Fair. The Piepowder court derives its name from the French for 'dusty foot', a reference to the court of the traveller. It provided justice for merchants and travellers from outside the borough when attending the town's fairs and markets.

The third court was the Durneday court, which appears to be unique to Bridgwater. Its purpose was to ensure that the citizens or burgesses paid their tolls and rents, Durneday being the day on which the

payment, perhaps for the lease of a burgage, became due, normally a day in January or February. Failure to pay the due amount resulted in the court ordering the door of the miscreant's dwelling to be sealed until such time as the payment was settled. 'Durn' is the old Somerset word for the frame of a door and is still, albeit rarely these days, used by carpenters of the old breed. Offenders had their doors sealed from one durn to the other, hence the Durneday court. In 1468, there was a new charter for the borough and it appears that the three courts effectively became one. In 1847 many of the functions of the court passed to the county court, and it finally became extinct with the Courts Act of 1971.

A rich example of the activities of the borough court is given to us by the records of the Michaelmas court of October 1378, in which the jury of 12 imposed punishments on all 195 of the brewers in the town, at least some of these because their ale was too bad, and on various others for offences such as:

Breach of the peace	Blocking the town ditch
Trespass	Cutting grass without consent
Having open drains	Leaving rubbish in the streets
Debt	Increasing the price of fish
Dumping animal skins and horns on the river bank	

An interesting feature of the early-medieval period was the almost complete lack of taxation as we know it today. Compared to modern times, where there are hundreds of employees of the local authority whose salaries have to be paid, in medieval times officials elected into various roles were unpaid, indeed were fined if they failed to fulfil their roles. If a bridge needed to be repaired, then the crown would first have to grant permission for a pontage to be raised, i.e. a tax to pay for the bridge which was raised from within the community of burgesses.

Borough archives from the early 1400s give an interesting insight into the way law and order was applied. Although the borough had two constables and two bailiffs to collect fines, the maintenance of peace and good order was the responsibility of individuals living within the borough. Each individual was expected to take his turn at maintaining vigilance in the town. One archived document contains a list of 279 names showing fines ranging from 1d. to 4d. (overwhelmingly the latter) imposed on those who failed to keep their watch. 'Vigilant' is marked against 55 names, showing that they had fulfilled their duty. Thus it tended to be the wealthy who paid to avoid such duty and the poor who were obliged to fulfil it.

The same archives show us that life was not all work and no play. In the 1450s we can see that at the yearly festival of Corpus Christi, gifts of wine were made to St John's Hospital, the Grey Friars and the vicar of St Mary's. On one occasions, pipers from Ash Priors were paid to add some entertainment to the occasion, although the town had its own piper, a fact that is known from records of the borough having paid for his coat. The Grey Friars also received two oxen from the duchess of Exeter.

Members of Parliament

In 1295, Bridgwater was called upon to send two burgesses to represent the town in Parliament. This was a dubious honour and most of those called on to attend were reluctant, there being little benefit, only inconvenience and expense to themselves, albeit they could claim for travel and accommodation. The journey from Bridgwater to London would have been very difficult in those days, travelling along green tracks for almost the entire journey. From 1298 Bridgwater had a good record for the attendance of its two representatives. The king would decide at any time which boroughs were to send representatives and most managed to escape the duty.

The Medieval Layout of the Town

Although the entrances to the town were gates, one at each point of the compass, the town was not walled. Rather it was contained within a series of ditches, rows of houses and the Durleigh Brook. Within the roughly oval shape, in the year 1444, were contained the following:

Eastover 58 houses	St Mary Street 51
Friarn Street 43	North Street* 39
South Street* 25	Castle Ditch 25
Fore Street 20	West Street 19
Orloffe Street 18	Damyate 1

The population at the time was about 1,600. Note that the High Street is not mentioned. This is because the street was so wide that it had an island down the middle and was classed as two thoroughfares, North Street and South Street, not to be confused with the present North Street which, in medieval times, was known as the Kidsbury or Wembdon way. The island in the middle of the High Street included the Cornchepyng, the corn exchange, and near that was the Cokenrewe with the Tolsey or toll-house. This cluster of buildings would have been more or less where the current Town Hall stands. 'Twixt church and Bridge' became known as Fore Street in 1367.

Dampiet Street was then Damyate, or the way by the dam. The dam would have been on the town brook, where corn was ground, at the Little Mill. Silver Street was known as 'Twixt the parish church and Friars Minor'. Horsepond Lane, in the same area, was known as 'Weyhur', which translates as horse pond. Eastover gained its name in 1357, prior to which it was 'Twixt Hospital and Bridge'.

Clare Street was Orloue (or Orfaire) Street and Market Street was Paynel Street, hence Penel Orlieu

being at the junction of the two. The origin of Orloue or Orfaire can be found in the Saxon word 'orf', meaning cattle. Orfaire was the cattle market, which fits perfectly, this being the area where cattle were sold right up to the 1920s. So this gives us the origin of Penel Orlieu. Understanding its origins, however, makes it no easier to spell!

There is a lovely story of a Bridgwater policeman who, when cycling past the Blue Boar Inn in Penel Orlieu was in collision with a drunk who was forcibly ejected from the inn right into the path of cycling constable. The officer picked himself up and took the drunk and the bike into the High Street, where the drunk was told to sit on a window ledge of the Duke of Monmouth Inn. There the officer informed him that he would be charged with drunk and disorderly behaviour outside the Duke of Monmouth in Bridgwater's High Street. When the drunk angrily reminded the officer that it was outside the Blue Boar that the incident had occurred, the officer asked the drunk if he could spell Penel Orlieu. They agreed to stick with the High Street as the place of the offence.

The relatively high number of houses in Eastover reflects the presence of a bridge across the river. William Brewer had seen the introduction of a bridge, albeit a wooden affair, and had actually started work on a three-arch stone bridge. This was lofty and wide, with houses on one or both sides. On the west bank a portcullis hung between massive towers with a drawbridge. A pathway ran along the quayside, passing under an arch which ran between the bridge and the houses. On Brewer's death in 1227 work came to a standstill. It was Sir Thomas Trivett who picked up the gauntlet and, with a donation of 300 marks, completed the task and fixed his coat of arms to the coping of the bridge. Although the bridge was sufficiently wide that it actually supported houses, heavy usage and strong tides took their toll and repairs were required in 1532 and 1678. In the same way that St John Street, Wellington Road, Devonshire Street and Edward Street were later to spring up with the advent of the railway, so Eastover sprang up with the easier crossing of the river.

In those early days, it appears that a bridge also existed serving the track between Hamp and Sydenham, almost certainly crossing the river at the same point that the Broadway bridge does today, where there was once a lime kiln, hence the name of the inn at that point. The chronicler Oldmixon refers to an old wooden bridge here in contrast to the Great Bridge, to which he also refers.

In 1538, Leland, the king's chronicler, visited the town and reported his finding as follows:

The way or I came into Bridgwater was caused with stone more than half a mile. Entering into Bridgwater I passed by a chapel of St Salvior standing in the ripe of the haven. Then I entered into a suburb and so over a

John Chubb's portrait of the High Street with its central row of buildings.. (From the Blake Museum)

John Chubb's impression of Binford Place and Trivett's Bridge. (From the Blake Museum)

bridge under which runneth a brook that risith a 4 miles of by West at Bromefelde. The south gate of the town joineth hard onto this bridge.

The town of Bridgwater is not walled nor hath been by any likelihood that I saw. Yet there be four gates in the town named as they be set. The walls of the stone-houses of the town be instead of the town walls. I rode from the south gate in a pretty street a while and then I turned east and came to the market place. The farrest street and principal show of the town is from westgate to eastgate. There is a right ancient and high bridge of three arches. That part of the town that standeth on the west side of the bridge and haven is three times as big as that that standeth on the east side. The castle sometime a right fair and strong piece of work but now all going to mere ruin standeth hard beneath the bridge of the west side of the haven.

In the Est part of the town is onely the House, late College of St John, a thing notable, and this house standeth partly without the est gate. This college had prestes that had the apparel of secular prestes, with a cross on the breste, and to this house adjoins an Hospice for poor folks.

In the west part of the town is a goodly house which had been the college of the Grey Friars

Trivett's bridge was clearly still standing and there is evidence that it lasted until 1795, when it was demolished and replaced with its iron-built successor.

The Churches and Religion

The Church of St Mary the Virgin

The Parish Church of St Mary the Virgin is certainly the oldest building in the town, largely built in the Early-English style but mixed with Decorated and Perpendicular. Internally, the archway leading to the tower appears to be Early English and from the early-thirteenth century. At the west and north sides of the nave, windows are set in Early-English casings.

The former vestry at St Mary's Church.
(FROM THE BRIDGWATER TOWN COUNCIL COLLECTION, COURTESY THE BLAKE MUSEUM)

Decorated windows of the fourteenth century can be found elsewhere, the remaining being fifteenth-century Perpendicular, indicating how the church was regularly undergoing change in its earlier years. The earliest record we have of a vicar is that of Richard, in 1280. In 1318–19, a great bell was cast. This being the case, it is safe to assume that the tower as we know it today, albeit without the spire, was existent before 1318. We know that William Brewer was re-building it in the early 1200s, on the site where Merleswain had his earlier Saxon timber church. In 1367 work commenced on the spire, built by Nicholas Waleys from Bristol. The work was slow, it being realised that the spire would be too heavy for the tower and that the tower would have to be strengthened by the addition of buttresses. In the 1440s, when the spire needed repair, Thomas Stipilman, presumably a steepleman or jack, was brought into the town for a ten-week stay. Around the same time, John Glayser was brought in from Wells to work on the church windows. In these names we can see how a person's trade was still the defining factor in their choice of surname.

The red stone of the 174ft high tower came from Wembdon and the fawn sandstone from Ham Hill, floated down the river on barges. It was from this tower that, in 1685, the Duke of Monmouth surveyed the king's troops camped at Westonzoyland. Indeed, the church was the last the Duke was ever to enter, as he was executed 11 days later. The nave is of Blue Lias from central Somerset roofed with lead from Wells. Within the grounds of the church were yew trees surrounded by stake fences to prevent pilferage of the branches, keenly sought for use as longbows. At one time the church grounds were also protected by iron railings running all the way around, but these disappeared when metal was required for the war effort. Within the church are eight bells, three medieval and five Elizabethan. A one-time vestry has long since disappeared.

The finances to maintain the church came partly from special collections and partly from levies and seat rental. Income also came from the chantries; St Mary's, founded by Isolda Parewastel; St George's and the Holy Trinity. At one time there were as many as six altars within the church; Our Lady, Trinity, St George, Holy Rood, St Katherine and the High Altar. Parishioners would each have their favourite altar and would light a candle before their chosen one, further helping with the revenues. In addition, in the late-fourteenth century, there was a charge of 3s.4d. for burial in the church grounds. Those who had wealth would leave a legacy to the church for prayers to be recited to ensure their souls went to heaven. Another form of fund-raising was through church ales, whereby ale was brewed and sold for the benefit of the church. These sales were as common as church bazaars today and fulfilled a similar function. However, by the 1450s, church ales were no longer a

fund raiser for St Mary's. Instead a tax was levied on the parishioners, the monies raised being used to buy timbers from Hamp and Enmore and lead from Axbridge and Bristol. Wax for the candles was another expense and worked out at 6d. a pound, the equivalent of a craftsman's pay for a day.

At the time of the Act of Supremacy, which passed control of the church to Henry VIII and away from Rome, St Mary's Church survived unscathed. Thomas Strete was the vicar and it must have been a difficult period for him as he watched the Grey Friars disappear and then the brothers of St John's, with nothing to replace the invaluable service these houses provided. Within his own church, the chantry priests disappeared, as did the nuns of Cannington. He would have worked closely with all of these communities, the links between the various religious groups being quite strong rather than well demarcated. Their disappearance would have saddened him but imagine his horror at the news in 1539 regarding the 80-year-old Abbot Whiting of Glastonbury. Whiting had resisted the change and paid with his life. Executed on Glastonbury Tor, he was hanged and then drawn. His head was then removed and displayed in Glastonbury whilst the rest of his body was quartered, a quarter being delivered by cart to Bridgwater, where it was stuck up contemptuously on the East Gate where the Cobblestones Inn now stands. Thomas Strete survived those difficult days and remained as the vicar at St Mary's through the reigns of Henry VIII, Edward VI, Mary and Elizabeth, passing away after 43 years in the role.

An act of God struck the church with near disastrous consequences in 1814. It was 7 November and the night of a great thunderstorm. At about half past seven in the morning there was a severe hailstorm with high winds. This was followed by a short period of calm and then, shortly after midday, the thunder began, increasing dramatically to a full-blown thunderstorm. The sky darkened, lit only by the frequent flashes of lightening. Then, in a blinding flash, there was an explosive crack as the church tower took a direct hit. The weather-cock was blown off and landed in Blacklands Fields. The repair was carried out the following year by Thomas Hutchings, a local builder. A series of poles were lashed together and rope ladders fixed to the spire. George Parker made the ascent to carry out the repairs. As part of the repairs, a lightning rod was fixed to avoid future disasters. The repairs were completed, the weather-cock replaced and the scaffolding removed. It was then realised that the weather-cock was not turning with the wind. A wedge which had been placed to stop the weather-cock turning during the repairs had been left in place. A kite was flown over the weather-cock and the string allowed to fall either side. A rope attached to the string was pulled over the top of the spire.

Scenes from the 1927 Pageant depicting the riots at St John's. An angry crowd gathers (top) *and a hostage is led away* (above). *Note Sydenham Manor House in the background* (above right).

(FROM THE ROGER EVANS COLLECTION)

Scenes from the 1927 Pageant: The brothers of St John's Hospital leave their premises, led by the rioters.
(FROM THE ROGER EVANS COLLECTION)

Then an experienced mariner by the name of Captain Gover climbed the rope as though he were climbing ships' rigging. Reaching the top, he removed the wedge and completed his safe descent.

St John's Hospital

It was not only the castle which William Brewer left as a legacy. Apart from an abbey at Dunkeswell and a castle at Torquay, in 1216 he built St John's Hospital in Bridgwater. This was an Augustine Priory, a gift confirmed by Bishop Jocelin in 1219 following a charter of 1213 which granted its founding with permission to use five acres of land to support 13 poor or infirm persons. It also served the needs of pilgrims but was closed to lunatics, lepers, epileptics, pregnant women, breast-feeding mothers and those with contagious diseases, no matter how sick or destitute. The rich and the powerful were also barred from taking lodging, entertainment or allowing their horses to feed there. Its main function was to provide food and lodgings for travellers, to care for the sick and to educate the young of the poor of the town.

It was a self-governing establishment, its master being elected from within its own brethren. Their attire was that of the common hospitallers, with the exception that they sported a large black cross on their mantles and outer garments. This distinguished them from the Franciscan friars, who were set up at the other side of the town. Part of their role was to serve the church of St Mary's and also to serve on a daily basis at services in the castle chapel. Three women 'of good fame' lived in the priory in order to attend the sick and infirm.

Based just outside the east gate, its position today would be at the start of Broadway by the entrance to Eastover. Within the grounds there was the 112ft long St Katharine's Church, an infirmary, rectory, dormitory, chapter house, cloister, parlour and a school, the first for Bridgwater. A herb and vegetable garden, a fish-pond for Friday dinners, and a graveyard completed the picture. In 1286 a licence was granted for a channel to be cut down to the river in order to clear waste from the privies. This was 3ft wide and of sufficient depth to allow the river to run all the way in. It was then covered over, presumably with timbers, so that earth and stone could be placed on top, allowing those whose land it passed through to cross it unhindered. A track running from the hospital up to the Polden Hills and known as the Long Causeway followed the line of Monmouth Street and Bath Road to Crandon Bridge, locally known as the Silver Fish. This may well have been a significant link to a priory which was once based at Horsey.

In 1298, Geoffrey de Mark, the first master of any note, had bound himself to maintain 13 live-in scholars. They lived and ate in the grounds but took their education in the town. The funding for their education came from Robert Burnell, Bishop of Bath and Wells, with funds from Morwenstow and Wembdon. In return, seven poor scholars from the town were fed at the priory. This arrangement continued until at least 1535, at which time the properties were surrendered to the king. During that time, between 1329 and 1336, Sir John Popham of Huntworth was one of the financial supporters and new buildings were added in 1350 and 1450. In 1349, the good works of the friars were recognised by the granting of 16 dwellings with the associated land, a shop, a cellar, a stall, a garden and 23½ acres of land. The establishment was growing in power. It was even granted control of the churches of St Mary's in Bridgwater, St George's in Wembdon in 1284, Northover, Isle Brewers, Chilton, Edstcok and others as far afield as Cornwall. Indeed, it became so powerful that in 1300 the master was summoned to perform military service against the Scots.

The Wat Tyler Rebellion and the Sacking of St John's Hospital

In 1349 the Black Death plagued the nation. The population of Bridgwater diminished by about a third. The nation was undermanned and the cost of labour rocketed, creating unrest which was to last for decades and which came to a head in 1381. It was a period which also gave the town the spire of St Mary's Church, assumed to be a token of thanksgiving from those who survived the plague. This gives the background for what happened next.

In 1380, Thomas, the master of St John's Hospital, complained that William Blacche, a tanner, John Thomas, a carpenter, John Kelly, a hosier, and many others, had attacked the hospital, breaking doors and windows and taking food and £20 in cash. They had locked all the doors, beat up the servants and threatened them in such a way that they were afraid to go back to the hospital. The event reflected the hostility which was developing between many of the locals and those who held power at the hospital. But it was only a prelude to what was to follow.

In 1381, the power held by St John's Hospital resulted in an unfortunate backlash. Across the country, but especially in the South East, there had been religious unrest which resulted in the troubles labelled the Wat Tyler Rebellion. The rebellion was crushed and Wat Tyler executed. In York, Scarborough and Bridgwater the news had failed to get through and the troubles continued. In Bridgwater, there was friction between St John's and St Mary's. St John's took all the tithes and even appointed the vicar of St Mary's. The master of St John's also had numerous deeds in respect of monies loaned to various townsfolk. Nicolas Frompton, a priest who had seen the way the Knights of St John had been treated in London, and Thomas Engilby, a yeoman, raised a mob of 14 men with Engilby as their captain. They forced their way into the house of the Knights and seized William Camel, the master, demanding that he transfer all properties and rights to Frompton. In addition, they burned a large number of deeds and bonds and bullied the master into signing a £200 ransom promise. Finished at the priory, they moved on to Sydenham Manor, home of John Sydenham, and burned the rolls of the manors of Sir James Audley and John Cole. Then they burned a tenement belonging to Thomas Duffield, and the house and goods of Walter Baron of East Chilton. Worse, they had Walter Baron beheaded.

On the Friday, Frompton headed towards Ilchester gaol, forcing John Bursy of Long Sutton to go with him. At Ilchester they removed Hugh Lavenham from the gaol and made John Bursy behead him so that they could take the head on a spear back to Bridgwater. There it was displayed on the Town Bridge alongside that of Walter Baron.

Then they heard the news that elsewhere the rebellion had been crushed several days before. This was bad news, Frompton and Engilby having used the rebellion as justification for their actions, though their grievance was, in reality, unrelated and a strictly local affair. Engilby fled the country and, in his absence, was condemned to death. Before the month was out he was pardoned. Frompton, meanwhile, had disappeared, never to be heard from again.

Further troubles occurred in 1463, when an auditor was sent in to investigate reports of misbehaviour by the brethren of St John's. There were so many of them found guilty of various crimes that additional dungeons and stocks had to be constructed. The following year, the bishop had to investigate claims of miracle cures at Wembdon. A well, called St John's Spring, provided water which everyone suddenly believed could cure various illnesses, but only if a financial offering was made. Masses of people visited, the revenue generated being such that the bishop could not bring himself to question its legitimacy as a place for miracles.

An entry in the diocesan registers for 1534 gives us a small insight into the hardships of the hospital. The bishop agreed to offer some relief to the brethren who attended the night services which, during bitter winters, had caused many of them to fall ill. It was agreed that they should not hold their first service until 5a.m., relaxed to 6a.m. during the winter months on condition that they first rang a bell to waken travellers, workmen and their neighbours in order that they might attend and receive God's blessing before commencing their day's work.

That same year, with the suppression of the monasteries, the hospital's days were numbered. The end was recorded as follows:

It was on a dark September evening, AD1534, that the inhabitants of Bridgwater were disturbed in their usual avocations by the entrance of a troop of the King's soldiers; this sight, however attractive and amusing in these days of peace and liberty, at the time of which we are speaking spread terror and alarm. The troops having paraded through the town, proceeded to the hospital, which opened its gates to receive them, and an officer stepping forward handed a letter, sealed with the royal arms of England, to Robert Walshe, its master. The supremacy question had just been mooted, and this was an order for the dissolution of the house if the King's authority were denied. A meeting in the chapter was soon convened, and twelve of their number was soon present. They wore the apparel of the order. Their consultation lasted but a short time, their course was clear, they knew resistance would be in vain, in fact they were aware that the object of this visit was their annihilation. They therefore soon decided that rather than their house, which had been dedicated to God, should be desecrated by the mercenary band now in its courtyard, it would be better to admit the King's supremacy. Accordingly they all signed the document presented, and the officer thus satisfied soon retraced his steps towards London.

Though the religious body disappeared it survives in the name of St John Street. At one time a large piece of an ornate window, a surviving remnant of St John's Hospital, served for many years as an ornament outside Hamlin's Garage in Monmouth Street. It apparently later disappeared, having been handed over to the town's museum.

The disappearance of the Augustine friars left a huge gap in terms of education. St John's appears to have been the only recognised centre of learning. Henry VIII's dissolution left Bridgwater without formal education and it was not until Queen Elizabeth endowed a free grammar school with an annual payment of £6.13s.4d. for the youth of the town and neighbouring parishes, that education returned. Richard Castleman enhanced this in 1633 with an endowment, as did George Crane and Mrs Brent in 1699.

Whilst Henry VIII's Act of Supremacy had a detrimental impact on many towns, he smiled kindly on Bridgwater for some unknown reason. He bestowed upon the town the peculiar honour of county status. One effect of this was that the county sheriff would no longer be able to serve a writ on the town, and herein may lie the reason for the change in status. However, the benefits of the honour were never taken up.

The Grey Friars of Friarn Street

Around 1230, following in his father's footsteps, William Brewer's son, also William, who served with distinction in the crusades, opened the Grey Friars', or Friar Minor's, Franciscan priory in Friarn Street. It appears that the priory building was probably built some time later. The land had been donated in 1246 and the king granted Richard de Plessy, the keeper of the parks, permission for five oak trees to be taken from North Petherton forest to be used as timber in building the priory. These were felled in 1250, 1278 and again in 1284, suggesting gradual expansion. The low-lying meadows along Durleigh Brook formed part of the property of the priory. Hamp Brook probably formed another boundary since in 1371 the Friars Minor had to answer a complaint that they had failed to keep the brook clean. The building itself was '10 steppys' in length, about 210ft. An old arched doorway in Silver Street is believed to be the sole relic of this long-vanished priory. Recent archaeological exploration has given us confirmation of the site and size of the establishment.

Among its early benefactors were William of Worcester and Roger Mortimer. For 300 years, the Franciscan Friars served the community, dedicated to improving the lives of others, especially the sick and destitute. They practised chastity and poverty and were easily distinguished from the Augustines by their much simpler attire. The Franciscans wore grey hooded gowns, girded with a cord. They travelled barefoot and took no money, only gifts of food and medicines, as they wandered the countryside serving the community and preaching the gospel, which they were only permitted to do so by way of licence. In contrast to the Augustine Friars who moved very little from their St John's base, the Grey Friars travelled far and wide, reaching people in need, and through their deeds became very popular. They also received gifts in the form of bequests in wills. Since their order was denied financial offerings, the gifts were of a practical nature, such as that of William Dyst, who left them four bushels of green peas. Others left wheat, beans and a 12-gallon vat. A well-to-do lady bequeathed them her best gown with grey fur and her best girdle harnessed with silver and gilt. In later years the rules were relaxed and they were permitted to receive financial aid, but fundamentally for the upkeep of their premises and not for their personal improvement.

They were mostly, but not all, learned men, who helped in the writing of wills as well as tending the sick and destitute. Amongst their number was an exceptional man, Brother John Somer, an amazing astronomer who wrote an astronomical calendar for Joan, Princess of Wales, wife of the Black Prince. Geoffrey Chaucer, the first English poet, in writing a poem for his son, made reference to John Somer and the astronomical calendar he produced. Somer had been educated at Oxford and excelled in philosophy and mathematics, being considered unequalled anywhere in the realm. It was for his writings on astronomy that he is best remembered, having learned from the writings of others but having added much new material of his own. Around 1390 he published *Canons of the Stars, Of the Quantity of the Year, Corrections of the Calendar*, along with many other works which were to bring him fame.

The Franciscan establishment in Friarn Street survived until the suppression of the monasteries under Henry VIII. It was a sad end to the dedicated brotherhood who had quietly and humbly served the parish so well. But when the Act of Supremacy was introduced the humble Grey Friars were the easiest local target and hence the first to go. They were helpless and signed the deed of surrender, which I translate as follows:

Memorandum: We the warden and convent of the Grey Friars of Bridgwater with one assent and consent, without any manner of coercion or counsel, do give our house into the hands of the lord visitor to the king's use desiring his grace to be good and gracious to us. In witness we subscribe our names with our proper hands the thirteenth day of September in the 30th year of King Henry VIII.
Signed: John Herys Thomas Howeett John Wake
Richard Harris John Cogyn Andrew Gocyt
Robert Oliver Gerard Morley

It is highly unlikely that the Grey Friars gave up their premises as readily as the 'without any manner of coercion or counsel' would suggest. Like a turkey voting for Christmas, signing the deed left them with no roof over their heads, no personal belongings, and wandering the streets, barefoot and unemployed. Whilst some churches perhaps deserved what was coming, the Grey Friars deserved better. The financial benefit to the king was minimal, but the loss of the service provided by the brothers was enormous. From the building itself, the lead from the windows was probably the most valuable asset. The other items were those associated with their worship: a table, altar cloth, two candlesticks, a pair of organs, a sacristy bell, three cloths, an iron frame around a tomb, an old coffer and a few items of clothing. Emanuel Lucar purchased the site and that was the end of the Grey Friars.

There are also records of a Hospital of St Giles which existed from the mid-1300s to 1539. Little is known of this establishment other than that it started as a leper colony and became a hospital sited just outside the old west gate.

Fair scene from the 1927 Pageant showing the reading of the charter.

(FROM THE ROGER EVANS COLLECTION)

A fair scene from the 1927 Pageant with a dancing bear.

(FROM THE ROGER EVANS COLLECTION)

CHAPTER 3

Fairs, Markets and General Trade

The Earliest Fairs

The vibrancy of any town could be measured by the success or otherwise of its fairs and markets. In the mid-thirteenth century Bridgwater, with its 300 burgages, had 13 stalls and five shops. It also had three Jews, only two of whom were licensed to act as bankers and money lenders. These were Bateman, who was resident, and Mampson, who appeared to be more a seasonal visitor. The third Jew, Koket, had been fined for trespass. Goldsmiths, wine merchants and all those trades associated with the wool industry were to be found.

The earliest record we have of a fair is the eight-day fair granted by King John in the charter of AD1200, starting on 24 June. It survived until its quiet disappearance in 1357. The following year, other fairs took its place. The Ascension Fair, held when cherries were in season, survived until around 1900, by which time it had become a shoe and cloth fair. There was a midsummer horse and shoe fair, which was originally held in George Lane and then moved to Dampiet Street. Records of 1831 refer to it as the smallest of fairs, predominantly trading cart horses, with some trade in beef and lamb. The same year the Lent Fair is reported. Held on the second Thursday in Lent, it commenced in 1468 and traded in cows, calves, cheese, bacon and cloth. The Christmas Fair, with similar commodities, was held on 27 or 28 December. A summer horse fair, held in Eastover, raised funds for St John's Hospital and lasted until the early 1900s.

St Matthew's Fair

The fair which survives today is the gigantic St Matthew's Fair, which dates back to 1249. Its charter was renewed in 1613. For centuries it has been a high spot in the social calendar and has been held on the same site for most of that time. Originally held in the centre of the town, by 1404 it had grown so large it was moved to St Matthew's Field and West Street. Once held on 21 September, it now commences on the last Wednesday in September and lasts for four days. It was a one-day fair until 1857, when a local Act was passed to make it three days. Then, in 1919, the weather was so disastrous that a fourth day was granted to help the traders and it has remained as four days ever since.

Today it is significant as a funfair but it once served as a hiring fair, at which large numbers of sheep and ponies were sold, many of them having

Monmouth Street and the horse fair of 1906. (FROM THE ROGER EVANS COLLECTION)

been rounded up in the Quantock Hills. In 1881 there were 700 horses and ponies on sale. In 1893 nearly 5,000 sheep were auctioned. Four years later, in 1897, there were three auctioneers who between them sold hundreds of horses and around 7,000 ewes. The problem was that they achieved this in torrential rain and the field was left a quagmire, having been trampled by around 8,000 sheep and ponies.

Historically the fair has great social significance. Seldom during the farming year would farm labourers have the opportunity to leave their place of employment or go beyond the bounds of the village in which they lived. Well-to-do families would rent a house in the town for a week. Working families could go to the fair, hire themselves out individually, and end up scattered around the county, not seeing each other until the next Bridgwater Fair. Men and women would line themselves up for sale, each carrying the tools of their trade; the shepherd with his crook, the stockman with his whip, the milkmaid with her stool. During the nineteenth century, the Thursday of the fair became known as 'Servant's Day', this being the day when shop workers would take up new employment, the Friday night being for factory and domestic workers. The fair has also been a traditional gathering place for Romany gypsies, in like fashion to Priddy Sheep Fair, where perhaps again it is the pony sales which are the attraction.

Wife Sales

Apart from the social aspect, trade was vitally important. Imagine not leaving your village to go shopping other than that once-a-year trip to the fair.

The pots and pans, rolls of cloth, boots and shoes, hats, coats, tools and all the other items except day-to-day food could be bought at the fair. Perhaps it is no wonder that at one year's fair there were more than 150 stalls selling just boots and shoes. You could buy and sell almost anything at the fair, even a wife, as was witnessed in 1761 in the case of John and Betty Bodger. Betty had produced no children, so John took her to the fair and there she was sold by auction for the sum of £5 to James Bacon, a widower and fisherman of Stogursey. Two years later the couple married in Stogursey Church and produced seven children. In the county archives there is the deed of sale which reads as follows:

I, John Bodger, this eighth day of November 1761 have and do and for divers causes and lawful reasons moving me thereunto let and set and entirely sell all my right and property in Betty Bolt, otherwise Betty Bodger, my lawful wife, as it appears by the register of the parish church of Taunton St James in the County of Somerset, unto James Bacon of the parish of Stogursey, fisherman, to have and to hold as his lawful wife for evermore. And I the said John Bodger, do promise and assure the said James Bacon that, on penalty or forfeiture of £10 of good and lawful money of Great Britain, I will never claim or make any demand or demands on the said Betty Bolt or her new husband the aforesaid James Bacon.

Signed with the marks of all three parties.

Thieves, Rogues and Vagabonds

Such an abundance of trade at a fair will inevitably attract a number of thieves, rogues and vagabonds.

West Street during Bridgwater Fair in the 1950s.　　　(From the Roger Evans Collection)

One such vagabond was Bampfylde Moore Carew who, although born a gentleman, preferred the life of a traveller and was known as the King of the Gypsies. He was a master of disguise and an accomplished confidence trickster. He turned up at Bridgwater Fair somewhere around 1730 with a gang of conmen, each with a disguise: a cripple, a blind man, an out-of-work sailor, and suchlike. The town mayor recognised Carew and had him and his gang imprisoned. The mayor simply wanted rid of them and did not want the trouble of a trial, so the gaoler was instructed to chat with the prisoners and let them know that the mayor was a cruel man who particularly hated conmen. He described the punishments the mayor had inflicted on earlier vagabonds. The gang swallowed the stories hook, line and sinker. When the gaoler 'accidentally' left the prison door unlocked, they made their escape, the cripple throwing away his crutches, the blind man miraculously regaining his sight, and they were never again seen anywhere near Bridgwater.

The problem of infestation by vagabonds continued and in 1832 the Bridgwater *Alfred* reported the recruitment of an additional 30 constables to deal with them. It seems they were very successful. After arresting the first three they met, the problem disappeared and the officers were able to turn their attention to illegal gamblers running such games as thimble-rigging and pricking the garter. Those caught gambling were swiftly dealt with by the local police, Bridgwater having its own force at the time.

Mummers and marionettes were amongst the more refined diversions and amongst the less

Coles Gondolas (above) *with a likeness of King George V* (top) *c.1960.* (FROM THE ROGER EVANS COLLECTION)

A boxing booth at Bridgwater Fair, 1958.

(FROM THE ROGER EVANS COLLECTION)

The striptease show at Bridgwater Fair, 1958.

(FROM THE ROGER EVANS COLLECTION)

The galloping horses at Bridgwater Fair, 1960.

(FROM THE ROGER EVANS COLLECTION)

The rotor at Bridgwater Fair, 1960. (FROM THE ROGER EVANS COLLECTION)

savoury were the menageries and freak shows. Emmanuel Dukes had a freak show with which he toured the country and in 1797 he added a new attraction on his visit to Bridgwater. The unfortunate Sarah Biffen was born in East Quantoxhead in 1784 with no arms, legs, hands or feet. Despite her disabilities, she had learned to read and write and to do needlework. As the daughter of an agricultural labouring family, her future was bleak and so her parents sold her to Emmanuel Dukes, with indentures which guaranteed her £5 per annum. She travelled with Dukes's freak show and became known as the 'Eighth Wonder of the World'. Aged 21, she learned to paint and in time became an accomplished artist, painting for four kings and queens of England before a disastrous marriage and failing health led to her death in poverty in Liverpool.

Until the mid-1800s, the fun side of the fair was

Phil Strong in 1960, seller of a rejuvenating mixture 'guaranteed' to enhance male potency. In the crowd are Malcolm Wright, Colin Bryant and David Baker. (FROM THE ROGER EVANS COLLECTION)

West Street at fair time in 1907 (above) *and 1960* (below).   (FROM THE ROGER EVANS COLLECTION)

Sheep auctions at Bridgwater Fair, 1996.
   (FROM THE ROGER EVANS COLLECTION)

limited to travelling entertainers, there being no fairground rides as we know them today. Amongst the many forms of entertainment and now long since extinct, were performing bears and wrestling. The bears would be tethered by the neck and made to dance. Even as late as 1893 there was a strongwoman act, in which the lady concerned would lift a horse, while in the adjoining sparring booth visitors were invited to wrestle with a bear. Apart from this unusual act, wrestling was a local affair, in which only men from Bridgwater or the surrounding villages were allowed to take part. They wrestled stripped to the waist and strict rules were applied whereby the opponent had to be thrown or pinned to the ground. In latter years these were replaced by the 'professional' wrestlers and boxers who performed in the booths, my father being one of them in his earlier years. He had learned to box in the Navy between the two world wars and was one-time boxing champion of the Yangtze River. Having left the Navy, he travelled the West Country with the fair during the summer months, visiting Plymouth, Barnstaple, Bideford and other places, but always finishing the season at Bridgwater before retiring for the winter, during which time he worked as a postman in Bridgwater.

Joe and Tom Wilson, one-time lightweight champions of England, appeared at Bridgwater, as did Freddie Mills and the Turpin brothers, whose names were renowned worldwide. Freddie Mills appeared at the fair from 1937 to 1939 and by 1948 had become World Light Heavyweight Champion.

Next to the boxing concession, which was owned by the McKeown family, there was the striptease tent, which usually needed a gimmick such as a knife-throwing act as part of the performance. 'Roll up, roll up, roll up. She's alive and showing on the inside,' the barker would shout. 'Eve without leaves. She wears nothing, absolutely nothing. Step inside, sir. Ladies especially welcome.' Night after night I would hear the owner of the show whipping up the crowd as I worked on the hoopla stall as a six-year-old whilst my father was in the boxing booth or taking money on the Jungle Ride.

Just along from the striptease tent was the beer tent, for decades the domain of Fred Cavill, licensee of the Hope Inn. Boxing and wrestling also took place on a nightly basis outside the beer tent but it was never for sport and often involved the gypsy families who took control of such outbreaks themselves, needing no help from the local community.

By the 1860s, fun rides, propelled by ponies or young lads, were a regular feature, with swing boats and roundabout horses, but there were none of the high-speed daredevil rides of today. Mostly the amusements were penny peep-shows and rather poor theatrical offerings inside canvas tents. There were equestrian displays, performing pigs and even

The position of the Cheese Cross immediately outside Marycourt, now the Carnival Inn.

(FROM THE ROGER EVANS COLLECTION)

Right: *The base of St Mary's Cross, which was moved to Penel Orlieu as the Pig Cross.*
(FROM THE ROGER EVANS COLLECTION)

Below: *The old market cross, at the Cornhill from the fourteenth century until 1827.*
(FROM THE ROGER EVANS COLLECTION)

a trained seal advertised as a talking fish! It was in the 1880s that mechanisation first appeared and then, in the 1890s, came electricity. Steam-powered Venetian gondolas made their first appearance, then a roundabout and in 1886 there were steam-driven galloping horses.

Such was the magnetic attraction of these spectacles that the popularity of the funfair grew dramatically and it was around this time that the original purpose of the fair as a place to trade sheep, ponies and other commodities, previously the mainstay of activity, were eclipsed. The introduction of new rides such as the big wheel in 1905 helped to speed up this process, though the travelling theatres and a circus still remained the principal crowd-pullers.

During the early-twentieth century, it had always been understood that the showmen could not enter the fairfield with their heavy traction engines until after midnight on the Sunday before the fair. During the rest of the year, the field was used for allotments and so the growers were obliged to clear their crops before the traction engines flattened them. In wet years, these heavy engines would often get bogged down in the mud and it was sometimes a case of waiting for drier weather before they could be extracted. Once midnight came, the traction engines would go at full speed up onto the fairground, and in

1910 four drivers were charged with breaking the two miles per hour speed limit for such engines, one driver even reaching three miles per hour!

Apart from the activity on the fairground, West Street has long provided the main focus for the sale of a wide range of commodities, from glass-cutters to fortune telling. It was also the centre of focus for sales of alcohol. During the period of the fair, anyone who lived along West Street could open their doors or windows for the sale of alcohol without a licence. These homes, known as 'Bush Houses', used their back rooms and bedrooms and anywhere that a customer could be squeezed in, until they were banned by law in the 1860s. In their time they greatly added to such existing licensed public houses as the Cardiff Arms, Halswell Inn and Nag's Head. The most noticeable items along the street were china, carpet and bulb sales and many of these traders were, and still are, reliable. Rogues existed in equal numbers, however; here today, gone tomorrow, until the introduction of the Consumer Act and similar legislation which clamped down on these individuals.

Throughout the twentieth century the funfair grew in size and took up more of the Fairfield as the livestock sales took up less. The Bioscope shows, once a regular feature, disappeared at the time that

Penel Orlieu cattle market, 1906. (FROM THE ROGER EVANS COLLECTION)

Above and right:
West Street sheep sales – note the sloping sides, c.1920
(FROM THE ROGER EVANS COLLECTION)

Colthurst & Symons brickyard barges moored up at the Langport slipway, c.1906.   (FROM THE ROGER EVANS COLLECTION)

the Bijou and Palace cinemas opened in the town. Gradually the theatrical acts also disappeared as new ideas developed. In 1921 Billy Butlin was at Bridgwater Fair with a single stall, which he transported by train. Five years later his entourage included five lorries and over 50 smartly uniformed employees. Then, in 1928, he brought the dodgems to Bridgwater Fair, and later created his holiday camp empire.

The foot and mouth crisis of 2001 brought an end to the sheep sales but the funfair and the associated West Street trading continue to be as popular as ever. The rides are becoming faster and now seem to focus on turning the visitor upside down rather than just spinning them around. It takes courage to venture onto these rides and I shall long remember a clever piece of marketing on one hair-raising ride. The sign simply said 'NO WIMPS'. What teenaged lad could walk past such a challenge – the queue was enormous.

Markets

Apart from the fairs, a regular market was held in Bridgwater, initially on a Saturday, at least until around 1600, and then latterly on a Wednesday. In St Mary Street there was a Cheese Cross, where cheeses were sold.

The cheese market was mostly supplied at the times of the various fairs. During the period of St Matthew's Fair, the cheese market had stalls stretching all the way down St Mary Street and into Dampiet Street, with hundreds of cheeses on sale. For some reason, in around 1800, the town council decided to move the cheese market into Friarn Street. The traders objected, moving their trade to Highbridge.

In 1857 an Act of Parliament rearranged the days of the town's markets and fairs as follows: the market on Wednesday instead of Thursday; St Matthew's Fair to the last Wednesday in September; Cock-hill Fair to the last Wednesday in January; Lent Fair to the last Wednesday in March; Midsummer Fair to the last Wednesday in June.

Fish, fowl, fruit and vegetables were sold in the Cornhill area. There were two market crosses in Bridgwater and one of these, known as the High Cross, was at the Cornhill in a position which would now place it in the middle of the road between the dome and the Lloyd's TSB bank premises. The cross, octagonal in shape, was used for the sale of various items but especially of fish. In 1694 a water tank was added to the roof to hold water for the town centre community. It was finally pulled down in 1827, having also served as a gallows at the time of the Monmouth Rebellion. It carried the interesting motto: 'Mind your own business'.

The other cross was the Pig Cross, a simple shaft with an orb atop, a replica of which can now be found at the Town Bridge end of Fore Street. The Pig Cross was at Penel Orlieu, where cattle and pigs were sold, sheep being sold in West Street, and was destroyed in 1830. It is believed that 'Pig' is not derived from the animal but rather from 'Pigens', an ancient manor which existed in the town.

Whilst market trading activity was once at the Cornhill, as buildings sprang up around the area, so the traders spread out along Fore Street, then known as 'Twixt church and bridge' and along the High Street, known as 'Great Street'. Indeed, it was such a great street that there was even room for a row of shops down the centre of the road and this accounts for the wide space across parts of the current High Street, reflecting the frontage of the old line of shops.

Trade

Surprisingly, there is very little evidence of wool being exported from Bridgwater in the thirteenth and fourteenth centuries. It appears that wool for export had to be taken to Wells for collection and transportation. An exception was in 1347, when the order was given that wool destined for the Italian firm of Bardi was to be taken to Bridgwater to be shipped from there.

During the fourteenth century, the Bridgwater cloth trade expanded considerably, not least because of the superior quality of locally made cloth, the speciality being a ratteen, a coarse serge-like cloth known as a 'Bridgwater'. Taunton and Dunster had reputations equal to Bridgwater and cheap imitations were a problem for local traders. It eventually became necessary to introduce legislation which made it illegal to sell 'Bridgwaters' in rolled-up form. The cloth had to be exposed so that the buyers could see that they were getting the real thing. In 1388, three traders from Taunton were caught illegally selling cloth at Bridgwater market; the following year Parliament introduced an Act which made such practices illegal.

To produce these fine cloths, teasels were required to raise the nap, and these grew in abundance, especially in the area around Isle Abbots and Isle Brewer. Much of Bridgwater's wealth was based on wool and cloths. This affluence helped the town to grow until the sixteenth century. When the export trade declined, as continental producers overtook the English in their processing and dying techniques, Edward III found a solution. To counteract this threat to the nation's exports, he bought in the skills required by recruiting Flemish workers who settled in Somerset and the position was recovered.

Within the walls of the castle there was a fulling mill, tuckers, dyers and carders. Outside the castle, the same businesses would be found in many cottages. There were also goldsmiths, indicating the wealth from the wool trade, and mercers, men who traded in cloth. The volume of trade was such that a new slipway on the river had to be built. This was the Langport slipway, built in 1488, paid for by the Abbot of Glastonbury, and is the slipway by the Town Bridge between the bridge and the library.

The statue of Robert Blake, Bridgwater's hero of the Civil War. (FROM THE ROGER EVANS COLLECTION)

✦ CHAPTER 4 ✦

The Troubled Days of the Seventeenth Century

Never in the history of Bridgwater has there been such a violent and disturbed period as the seventeenth century, with civil war, rebellion and plague. It began with the Gunpowder Plot of 1605 and the failure of Guy Fawkes to blow up Parliament. That event is, of course, still celebrated today in the spectacular Bridgwater Carnival, which was dealt with in the publication *Somerset Carnivals*. For the purposes of this volume, suffice it to say that a Catholic attempt to blow up a Protestant Parliament was just a taste of worse to come. It was also a period in which scores of people died when, in 1607, heavy flooding resulted from the breach of a sea wall at Burnham. The floods extended inland well beyond Bridgwater. Then, in 1625, the plague hit the town, and river traffic was brought to a standstill for fear of the plague spreading.

The prelude to this period began in 1605, when the Revd John Devenish was appointed vicar of St Mary's. A man of Puritan persuasion, he was right for Bridgwater which, in general, leaned the same way. He liked to lecture and to preach, and not just on a Sunday. This found disfavour with the bishop, who condemned him for preaching on weekdays, indeed on market day and in the church. Humphrey Blake, brother to Admiral Blake, was the church-warden and he was reprimanded for not reporting the vicar to the authorities.

Early in 1644, Devenish died and was succeeded by George Wotton, who was nominated by Charles I. He was soon expelled, probably for using the Prayer Book and for conducting services in the traditional fashion rather than the 'new way'. It was tough on Wotton who, with a family of six children, was made destitute, his only crime being to preach in the way he felt was appropriate. But at least he survived, unlike the many others who were imprisoned or killed at this time.

Of the 8,000 clergy evicted from their posts, only 800 returned to their former roles once the dust of the Civil War had settled. Wotton eventually returned to Bridgwater, where he died in the vicarage in 1669.

By January 1646, Humphrey Blake was mayor of the town. The council, under his leadership, appointed John Norman, a Puritan. Defying the king this way was no longer such a risk, Charles I having lost most of his power and the Commonwealth Parliament being in control. But we have leapt from 1644 to 1646, and in so doing missed one of the most significant years in the history of the town.

The English Civil War and the End of Bridgwater's Castle

In 1645, the English Civil War, the conflict between the Royalist supporters of the king and the Roundheads, who favoured Parliament, and in which Bridgwater's Admiral Blake played such a key role, visited the town. In April 1645 Prince Rupert, for the king, summoned a meeting at Bridgwater Castle of justices loyal to Charles I in order to co-ordinate their activities. By July, the Parliamentarian forces of General Sir Thomas Fairfax, Lieutenant-General Cromwell and Major-General Massey arrived at Bridgwater, where they reflected on the strategic significance of the Royalist-held Bridgwater Castle. They had just enjoyed a couple of days' rest encamped at Westonzoyland, having routed the Royalist forces, many of whom had made their way to the perceived safety of Bridgwater Castle, at Langport.

A group of Roundheads captured Sydenham Manor, a Royalist household, where 100 Royalist horse were captured and where the marks of cannon balls still remain in the walls. Another group took Hamp; and in the channel, Royalist ships were intercepted to stop supplies reaching the castle, which was under the control of its governor, Colonel Wyndham.

Meanwhile, Fairfax and Cromwell carried out a reconnaissance and found the castle well defended with 1,800 troops and 40 or more guns. There was also the problem of the significant moat. As the two men surveyed the scene, they drew the attention of Lady Christabella Wyndham, wife of the governor. Having heard that Cromwell was on the opposite bank of the river, she found herself a loaded musket, went to the ramparts of the castle, exposed one breast to her enemies and fired a shot at Cromwell. Her aim was somewhat off and she shot the officer's sergeant-at-arms.

Lady Wyndham later sent a messenger to Fairfax asking if he had received her 'love token'. But why should she expose one breast? The gesture was by way of an insult. She had been wet nurse to Charles II when he was the young Prince of Wales and was later to complete his education in the art of love-making, a service which, according to Antonia Fraser's autobiography of Charles II, took place within Bridgwater Castle just before his fifteenth birthday. The following year he would have his first serious affair, in Jersey, and was later to become famous for his numerous liaisons, including that with Nell Gwynne.

In Bridgwater Charles encountered once more his former nurse, Mrs Crystabella Wyndham, wife of the governor of the town. To Mrs Wyndham in Bridgwater, should probably be accorded the honour of having seduced her former nurseling, the Prince of Wales. By the sexual standards of the time, to play such a gracious role in the life of a young prince was more of a privilege than an offence. Charles was nearly fifteen. Certainly by the time of his arrival in Jersey a year later he was a fully fledged man in the physical sense, capable of a proper love affair.

From *Charles II*, by Antonia Fraser

But back to the troubles at Bridgwater. The two Parliamentarian officers, Fairfax and Cromwell, moved their forces closer while they crossed the river at Dunwear by boat to view the castle from the other direction. Unprepared and unaware of the power of the tidal bore, their small craft was almost overturned by the wave. Then an attempt to storm the castle by night, by filling the moat with faggots of wood, was foiled by the sheer depth of the moat. Several days later the decision was made to storm the castle. The Roundhead forces were all stationed on the Eastover side of the river, camped at Castle Fields and parading around East Bower and Horsey. On 20 July Massey took a contingent to attack the castle from the south as a diversionary tactic. Lieutenant-Colonel Hewson was to attack from the north-east. First, however, Eastover, being the area within the ditched defence, had to be captured. In the early morning Eastover was attacked, the Roundhead forces crossing the ditch from the Castle Fields side using floating bridges. Captain Reynolds crossed the ditch at St John's and took control of the east gate, lowering the drawbridge at the gate and capturing Eastover and 600 prisoners. His troops fought all the way to the river, pushing Sir John Stawell's Royalists back across the river bridge, which was then barricaded as the drawbridge was raised.

Up at the Cornhill and around the church, the Royalists were coming under fire from their own captured guns. Fairfax regrouped his troops and prepared for the next major assault. Heavy fire from the Roundheads on all sides forced the Royalists into the castle. When one part of the castle was captured, many of the troops changed allegiance and fought for the Roundheads.

Within the castle Wyndham fought back, his guns firing incendiaries into Eastover, where all but three or four houses were razed to the ground. This accounts for the complete lack of any houses dating from before 1654 in that part of the town. Fairfax twice called unsuccessfully for the Royalists to surrender. Mrs Wyndham, clutching her bosom, told his messenger, 'Tell your masters that the breast which gave suck to Prince Charles shall never be at their mercy; we will hold the town to the last!'. The following day, Fairfax's troops prepared to storm the

castle, Fairfax first offering safe passage to the women and children within. As many as 800 took advantage of the offer, including Mrs Wyndham.

When battle commenced and the besiegers redoubled the cannonade, fires took hold all over the town, fanned by high winds. Wyndham realised the futility of continuing the defence. With 15,000 Roundheads outside the castle, the outcome was inevitable and prolonging the battle would simply cause more destruction. He offered the following terms of surrender:

1. *That the governor and officers might march away with their horses and pistols; and the common soldiers with their arms and have safe passage to Exeter.*
2. *That the inhabitants of the town may also stay or have liberty to go with them.*
3. *That the like liberty may be granted unto the clergy.*

Fairfax's reply, which Wyndham conceded was:

1. *That all should have quarter of their lives.*
2. *That the soldiers should march out without being stripped of their clothes.*
3. *That the townsmen shall enjoy their habitation without plunder.*
4. *That gentlemen and others should all be left to Parliament to dispose of.*
5. *That hostages should be sent only.*

By the evening of 23 July, it was all over. A total of 1,500 soldiers and 120 officers, 'a goodly store of fat priests' and two bishops had been taken prisoner, along with two months' supply of food and ammunition. Also captured were 5,000 weapons, 800 horses, 36 cannons and £100,000 of various valuables, these latter items having been taken to the castle for safe keeping. Five days later, Fairfax wrote to the Speaker of the House of Commons:

Mr Speaker, I dispatch hence letters of yesterday to the counties of both kingdoms, which gave some account of God's blessing on our endeavours in the storming of Bridgwater.

On Monday morning last, we gained that part of the town which lies this side of the river, and therein above six hundred prisoners, divers officers of quality, and two pieces of ordnance. The enemy fired that part of the town wherein we were and the next day burned down all the houses except two or three. Yesterday, perceiving an obstinate resolution in the enemy not to yield the town, I was forced to use those extremities for the reducing of it, which brought on a parley; and in short, to yield the town upon no other terms than quarter.

We entered the town this day, finding great store of arms and ammunition; thirty eight pieces of ordnance; above a thousand prisoners, and among them divers persons of great quality, as you will perceive by the list enclosed. I have not much time to spend here, and

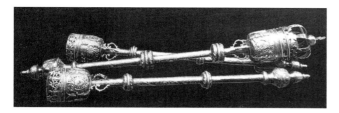

The three Bridgwater maces.

(FROM THE ROGER EVANS COLLECTION)

therefore shall dispose the command of it for the present to Colonel Rich, as Governor, wherein I doubt not of your approbation; and I believe the Commissioners of the Army will offer something further concerning him, and for the future settlement of the place. He is a gentleman of known and integrity; and his regiment at present with Major-General Massey: and I will, I believe, with God's blessing, give you a good account of it.

There was found in the town a commission from Prince Charles for ...... Phellips, a gentleman of this county, to raise a regiment of clubmen, which I send to you by Mr Peters. I am very desirous to give some encouragement to the soldiers for their many services, and especially for the honest and sober demeanour towards the prisoners of the town, in repairing the

Doug Moles, Bridgwater's long-serving current (2002) mace bearer. (FROM THE ROGER EVANS COLLECTION)

violence and injury, which has somehow brought dishonour upon most of the armies of this kingdom; which gives encouragement to them in the like for the future. I make no doubt that they will be well satisfied in what I shall do, and I assure you will be done with as little burden to the state as may be. I beseech to take into your consideration the necessities of the army, for a speedy supply of money, clothes, and other provisions; wherewith the bearer, Master Peters, will more particularly acquaint you more largely on all particulars of this late action, that I can now write.

Your most obedient servant, Thomas Fairfax

Eastover had been destroyed. Across the river, half the town had been ruined and in 1877, in the Barclay Street area, excavations uncovered a high mound of earth in which were buried human remains, bullets, swords and a variety of weapons.

In 1646, Parliament agreed to the destruction of Bridgwater Castle. In November of that year a troop of horse entered the town to commence its demolition. A battle broke out between the troops and the townsfolk, who wanted the destruction to go even further than instructed. After several deaths, the locals were suppressed and the demolition commenced. Probably the person who suffered the most from the destruction of the castle was Henry Harvey. The owner of the property at the time, he had leased it for two years to Edmund Wyndham. Mr Harvey's losses are described in the Harvey family archives as follows:

20 dwelling houses, 1 inn, 1 pigeon house of stone and 30 gardens pulled down and laid to waste; 1 barn, 2 stables and 150 bushels of corn all burnt to the ground; Mr Harvey's own home which was so battered it would cost £200 to repair; the goods and household stuff of the castle, all lost and will cost £100 to replace; £80 in unpaid rent for the castle for the two years and £15 loaned by him; 3,000 hogshead of castle lime, 1 fat ox and 5 fat oxen worth £50; 10 horses; 8 oxen and 8 cows; a 20 Mark debt and 18 sheep.

It just goes to show that before you rent out property, you need to know who you're dealing with!

After the Civil War, in 1657, Bridgwater was keen to show loyalty to the Commonwealth Parliament under its Lord Protector, Oliver Cromwell, for which purpose the town had three maces made which are now held in the town's silver collection. The large mace is 38in. long and of silver parcel gilt. It cost £25.10s.6d., and when Bridgwater failed to pay the silversmith on Ludgate Hill, he wrote to the Blake family and asked them to use their influence with the mayor to obtain the payment. Soon after, in 1660, Charles II came to the throne – inconvenient for a town whose mace demonstrated their loyalty to Parliament. By now Cromwell was dead and Charles II was in control – and so a crown was added

Admiral Blake's birthplace in 1904 – now the town's museum.

Blake's house as it looked in the sixteenth century.
(COURTESY CHRIS SIDAWAY)

to the top of the mace and an acorn to the base to demonstrate the change of allegiance. Close examination shows that the additions were not made to the same high standard as the rest of the piece. However, Charles must have been satisfied since he then granted the town four new fairs.

The origin of the mace dates back to medieval times, when a lord or king would have his champion lead his way, bearing a mace as a cavalry officer might carry a sword. It was a weapon which became a ceremonial item. Bridgwater's mayor is still preceded by his mace bearer on formal occasions.

The Town Silver

The two other town maces also date from the Commonwealth period. On the occasion of the royal visit to Bridgwater of Her Majesty Queen Elizabeth II and the Duke of Edinburgh, they visited the Town Hall, where the town silverware was on display. Bill Chedgey, a great Bridgwater character, was standing by the Great Mace when the Queen asked, 'What have you there?' Bill replied, 'Commonwealth maces.' Prince Philip turned to Bill's wife and said, 'I suppose you'll flog these tonight!'. 'Of course not,' replied Mrs Chedgey. 'Those are the raffle prizes. If you want one, you'll have to buy a ticket like everyone else!' The town silver collection contains numerous items: a 1663 silver salt cellar weighing almost 3lbs; a pair of 8in. high silver wine cups dated 1640; a 1675 silver sealing spoon, made in Bridgwater by Silver Street's Anthony Tripe and many other fine items.

Admiral Blake

Robert Blake was born in Bridgwater in August 1598, the eldest son of Humphrey and Sarah Blake. His home was the house in which the Blake Museum is now housed, in the appropriately named Blake Street. Baptised on 27 September at St Mary's Church, in the font which survives to this day, he was the first of 13 children, four of whom died in infancy,

leaving Bridget as the only girl. Their father was a local merchant who dealt in overseas trade, giving the young Robert an early introduction to the ways of the sea and the life of sailors. It is believed that it was one of Humphrey Blake's ships which first brought back the news of the advancing Spanish Armada. At the ensuing battle, the Bridgwater ship *William*, with its crew of 30, was under the command of Captain John Smyth.

The Blake family were comfortably off. Robert Blake's great-grandfather had property at Over Stowey. His mother had inherited land almost next door at Plainsfield, but it was his grandfather who left Plainsfield, moving to Bridgwater to run his import-export business, with four ships trading abroad by 1580.

Blake was educated at King James Grammar School in the town until the age of 16, when he attended St Alban's Hall and then Wadham College, Oxford. Whilst there he spent much time pursuing his passions of fishing and wild-fowling, skills undoubtedly learned on the moors and wetlands of Somerset. After nine years, Blake returned on instructions from his family. His father was close to financial ruin thanks to the Spanish Wars. The following year, his father died and Robert Blake assumed the role of head of the family. After selling part of the estate, there was still enough to survive on and to put his sister and youngest brother through their schooling. He had to abandon his own learning, however, entering instead the world of politics. Before that he disappeared for nine years, from 1629 to 1638, possibly working with his brother George and sister Bridget, who had moved to Plymouth and were running a shipping business there. It appears that during this period he spent some time in Holland but returned to Bridgwater on the death of his mother in 1638. It was a time when the country was divided between those who supported the Catholic king and those who supported a Puritan Parliament. Blake's younger brother had already emigrated to America due to persecution of his preferred style of religious practice. The family were devoutly Puritan.

Against this background, in 1640, Blake stood for Parliament and was elected. His time as an MP for the town was short-lived. King Charles, angered at Parliament's reluctance to give him as much finance as he requested, terminated the session but not before it had provided Blake with the opportunity to acquaint himself with Cromwell and other members of the Reform Party.

At the next election, Blake was defeated by the Royalist Colonel Wyndham, governor of Bridgwater Castle. However, an enquiry into a scandal involving Wyndham and a soap manufacturing and supply monopoly resulted in his losing his seat. The Civil War, meanwhile, was bubbling beneath the surface and Blake set about organising and training troops

Robert Blake returns to Bridgwater – a scene from the 1927 Pageant. (FROM THE ROGER EVANS COLLECTION)

for the Parliamentarian cause. Military success quickly came his way as the nation descended into conflict, and he won battles at Bodmin and Bath, with success at the siege of Bristol. This latter event, in July 1643, was a disaster for the Parliamentarian cause, the Royalists capturing Bristol. It was a success for Blake, however, whose garrison held out long after others had surrendered. It was this stubborn determination which earned him the rank of Lieutenant-Colonel.

His personal success at Bristol was followed by further glory at Lyme (Regis). The small Roundhead garrison there, little more than 1,000 men, had been harassing nearby Royalist towns and had attracted the attention of a unit of 6,000 Royalists who were preparing for an assault. Blake arrived and, although he was only number three in the chain of command, he offered the Royalist Prince Maurice the opportunity to settle the matter with the minimum of bloodshed. 'You send out 12 of your men, and I'll send out 12 of mine.' The offer was declined and the siege commenced. That the Royalists were making no impression was mostly down to Blake's leadership skills. After a week of siege, the Royalists attacked once more, breached the wall and gained access for many of their troops, whereupon Blake's men closed the gap, trapping hundreds of Royalists inside.

Part of the reason for the failure of the siege being that Lyme could be supplied from the sea, Prince Rupert attacked the Cobb, where the ships moored, sinking every vessel. Weeks passed in which siege and attack were repeated – but Blake resolutely led the defence until, several weeks later, Colonel Essex was

reported as advancing with fresh Parliamentarian forces, and Prince Rupert withdrew. Blake was declared a hero and packed off to Taunton.

Taunton was held by the Royalists but Blake was soon to capture it. He recruited and trained his own men, mostly Somerset men who he knew he could trust. It was with those forces that he captured and then held Taunton Castle through three separate sieges, with Colonel Wyndham once again his Royalist adversary. Between these sieges, his forces would harass any Royalist troops moving in the area. Blake was a thorn in their side. Taunton was not a strategic target, unlike Bridgwater, but as long as Blake held out, he served as a beacon to the Parliamentarian cause. During the sieges, he tied up three times as many Royalists troops as he had Parliamentarian ones. In one siege, the Royalists bombarded the castle for four days and hand-to-hand fighting in the streets preceded a tactical withdrawal to within the confines of the castle. Once again, Blake held out for weeks on end until re-enforcements arrived to relieve the position and the Royalists retreated to Bridgwater Castle, where it was their turn to be besieged.

After the fall of Bridgwater, Blake was sent to capture Dunster Castle, governed by Colonel Francis Wyndham, brother of the defeated governor of Bridgwater Castle. It soon became apparent that the capture of Dunster was beyond even the ability of Blake. His meagre force of 600, outnumbered three to one, could never take such a defensible position. Instead he moved to Barnstaple. The Royalists there, realising that Blake had come to attack their position, and perhaps overawed by his reputation, surrendered the castle. The Royalist cause was in a state of collapse. Blake returned to Dunster, where the Royalists were by then ready to surrender. The war effectively over, Blake returned to Bridgwater to become its MP.

Within three years there was more civil unrest in the second, albeit lesser, Civil War. The Navy was divided, part of it still loyal to the Crown, the other part to Parliament. What was left of the Navy was in serious need of reorganisation. Blake and two of his most trusted friends, Richard Deane and Edward Popham, were jointly appointed Generals-at-Sea, and as such introduced new ways of working. For the first time, men could be promoted from within the ranks, rather than being politically appointed. This meant that in time the most able would become the most senior officers.

With their revitalised, albeit small, Navy, they set about the capture of the Royalist fleet, action which included a siege at Kinsale in southern Ireland. There Blake's ships waited in rough seas for months, pinning down the Royalists, under Prince Rupert, until a violent storm drove them to shelter in Wales. It was another demonstration of the dogged determination of the Bridgwater man. At this stage, Cromwell felt that he was not making best use of Blake's incredible skills and he offered Blake overall command of the New Model Army. Blake declined, having taken on the task of rebuilding the Navy.

Blake tracked down the Royalist fleet, finding them in Lisbon harbour. Not wishing to upset the Portuguese, he bided his time. As the months passed, Parliament, concerned with the expense of keeping the fleet kicking their heels off the coast of Portugal, recalled the greater number of the ships and Blake's fleet was diminished to three. In order to overcome the problems this caused, Blake captured Portuguese ships on their way back from Brazil and used these to increase his fleet, and then did the same with the French, who had been attacking English ships. Prince Rupert, meanwhile, had slipped away. Once more Blake had to track him down, first to Spanish ports and then to the Canaries. Continually hounded by Blake's fleet, Prince Rupert's ships diminished in numbers, the final few eventually escaping to the West Indies. Blake returned to England, where the latest problem was that of the privateers based on the Isles of Scilly, Royalists among them, who were attacking English and Dutch shipping.

By the time Blake arrived at the Scillies, the Dutch commander, Van Tromp, was already waiting off the coast. Blake effectively had two enemies to deal with. A few days after arriving, Blake sent his sailors ashore, where they defeated the Royalists. He had instilled discipline in his sailors, training them to fight as well as any soldier. The Dutch went home, satisfied that the privateers had been dealt with. On Blake's return to England, he discovered that

Richard Deane was now with the Army, fighting in Scotland, and that Popham had died at sea. Blake was thus in sole command of the English Navy.

The naval successes which followed are well documented elsewhere. It is sufficient here to record that Blake continued to rebuild and improve the Navy, introducing welfare for sailors. With these better motivated crews he defeated the residual Royalist privateers in the Channel Islands, defeated the Dutch Navy under the command of Van Tromp and later de With, defeated the Barbary pirates and defeated the Spanish. During his many sea battles, in which his tactical abilities took maritime warfare into new territory, he received numerous wounds. At his final battle, at Santa Cruz, Tenerife, having sunk the Spanish silver plate fleet, he died. That last battle is perhaps worth recording here as just one example of this brilliant tactician's foresight and determination.

Blake had destroyed, or pinned down in Mediterranean backwaters, half the Spanish Navy. He knew the other half were on their way back from South America with silver to fund the war against England. It was vital that he stopped the fleet getting through. Acting on intelligence received, he sailed to the island of Tenerife, where he discovered the Spanish ships in the harbour of Santa Cruz, in a curved bay overlooked by high volcanic cliffs. On those cliffs were guns, ready to fire at intruders in the bay. Beneath the cliffs, in the shallower waters, was a curved line of Spanish frigates. Slightly further offshore, in the deeper waters, were Spanish men-o-war. The Spanish position was exceedingly well defended, cannon on the cliffs overlooking two lines of Spanish fighting ships.

Blake recognised the one weakness in this defence. It was no good attacking from offshore. To get close enough to engage the Spanish ships he would have to put his fleet in range of the guns on the cliff. If, however, he could get in between the two lines of ships, then the cannon on the cliff could not fire on his ships for fear of hitting their own. Similarly, if he was between the two lines of ships and Spanish ships fired on him and missed, they would most likely hit their own ships in the next line. His ships, moreover, could fire broadsides from both sides, attacking two lines at once.

As dawn broke he sent all his frigates into the fray, ordering them to sail between the two lines of Spanish vessels, knowing that the water would be deep enough for frigates, if not for the deeper-drafted men-o-war. At the end of a two-hour battle the Spanish fleet were all sunk or ablaze. It was an amazing success, but Blake's last. He died on the journey home of an accumulation of wounds from earlier battles and was given a hero's funeral. He was buried in Westminster Abbey, although Charles II later had his bones removed and thrown into a common pit. His heart and bowels had already been interred at St Andrew's Church in Plymouth.

In his will, Blake left £100 for the poor of Bridgwater; various sums of money to his brothers and sisters; his home plus another house in the town and 11 acres of meadow at Hamp to his brother Benjamin; a gold chain, various household items and sums of money to his cousins, nephews and nieces; and £50 for his negro servant, Domingo, to be used for his education and betterment.

He had never lost his love of Bridgwater and wherever his adventures took him, he always had Bridgwater men at hand. He is now remembered in Bridgwater at the Blake Museum, his birthplace, which was opened to the public in 1926. On one of the walls within the museum there is a sketch of a ship, possibly drawn by Blake or one of his siblings. Other memorabilia pertaining to Blake and other aspects of Bridgwater's past make this museum well worth a visit. Next to the museum are the remains of a building which housed an overshot mill, used in centuries past to grind corn for the castle.

Another memorial to Blake is his statue, which stands proudly in the town centre at the Cornhill. Built of hollow bronze by Mr Pomeroy, it cost £1,200 and was unveiled in 1900. Blake's name also lives on at Blake Gardens, positioned between the museum and the river, which were sold to the town by R.C. Else in 1898.

The Plague, a Suicide and an Ostracised Mayor

In 1665 the whole nation suffered from the plague, and Bridgwater was no exception. All over the country, people were afraid to enter towns for fear of infection, yet the food supply to the towns had to come from the country. Hence special arrangements were made. For Bridgwater, this meant that on the Bath Road, the country community would deliver farm produce and other wares as far as Horsey Lane and then venture no further. There they were met by the townsfolk, who kept a safe distance. An elm planted on the spot was known as 'Watch Elm'. Though hundreds died in the town, where they were buried is a mystery, some believing it to have been in a common grave, roughly opposite the current Town Hall in the High Street. What is known for certain is that there were no extra graves dug at St Mary's during that period. If the common grave theory is true, then those poor souls now lie beneath the shops built during the 1880s opposite the Town Hall.

In 1681 Robert Lush, a schoolmaster of Bridgwater, committed suicide. Though perhaps not that noteworthy, the fact that he was buried at night is a reflection of the attitude to suicide in the seventeenth century. In 1683, the struggle between Conformists and Nonconformists, and the struggle between church and politics continued. The mayor, William Masey, for the second time in three years, had berated the vicar of St Mary's for not paying sufficient to the

poor. However, the mayor left Bridgwater to take up residence in Ireland. With Masey now out of the way, the vicar made the following reference to him in the church register:

In the time of his mayoralty he commanded the minister to be rated to the poor, though it was never known in this parish, and when he was made mayor in this year in perfect spite, he commands it again. Whoever judges this man a lover of the church or anything that relates to it knows not the man. This man afterward carried himself with that insolency and tyranny to all sorts of people that the inhabitants, whether churchmen, Presbyterian, or other, joined together to ring out the belles for joy at his departure into Ireland, where he was preferred, and where it is thought he was poisoned.

The struggle that took place between Conformists and Nonconformists, mainly Presbyterians and Baptists, existed for decades. The Nonconformists included Quakers who, perhaps, suffered more than most. John Anderton, known and respected in the town as a well-to-do goldsmith, spent 20 years in prison for joining the Quaker society. Indeed, they continued to use his house for worship after his incarceration and were arrested as they made their way there, only to be released later at the vicar's request.

On the political front, Conformists were primarily Tory and Nonconformists primarily Whigs. The animosity between the two groups heightened during election times. Ralph Stawell of Cothelstone, a Tory candidate, described the Nonconformists as fanatics. After Stawell was twice defeated in his attempts to be elected to Parliament, he took his revenge on the Presbyterians and, in 1683, sent a troop of his militia to the site of the present Unitarian Chapel in Dampiet Street. There they stripped the old circular chapel of all its fixtures and fittings, which were taken to the Cornhill and used to create a huge bonfire, 14ft high, with the pulpit as the crowning glory. He then applied similar pressure to the local burgesses, bullying them into changing the rules which governed elections so that they would favour him in the future.

The Monmouth Rebellion

The final major turmoil for seventeenth-century Bridgwater came with the visitation of the Duke of Monmouth and the ensuing Battle of Sedgemoor. The greater part of the story takes place elsewhere and is adequately documented in numerous publications. Hence for the purposes of this volume, I shall focus on the impact on Bridgwater of this event.

James, Duke of Monmouth, was the illegitimate son of Charles II and Lucy Walter. Charles II had intended that Monmouth become the heir to the throne and had groomed him for that position.

Monmouth had been educated by a Scottish Protestant, who persuaded him that his parents were married and raised him as a Protestant in a Catholic environment. It became clear within the circles of influence within English politics that the king was grooming Monmouth and that, if he succeeded to the throne, there would be a Protestant king. Monmouth had carried out a West Country tour in 1680 and proved tremendously popular. Tens of thousands of West Country folk flocked to see him. The Catholic power base did all that was necessary to ensure he fell from grace with the king.

On the death of Charles II, his brother, James Duke of York, took the throne as King James II. Monmouth at this time was in Holland, in military service with William, Prince of Orange. France and England were now allied as Catholic nations, posing a threat to Protestant Holland and Monmouth, a potential target as pretender to the throne, for a while went into hiding. However, he was persuaded by his mistress, Lady Henrietta Wentworth, that his destiny was to be the Protestant King of England.

Monmouth and the Earl of Argyle plotted to create two simultaneous rebellions, Monmouth in the South West and Argyle in Scotland, both strongly Protestant areas. This would split the forces of James II. In June 1685 Argyle's attempt at rebellion in Scotland failed and he was beheaded. Monmouth, meanwhile, was on his way to Dorset, unaware of the failure of the rebellion in the north.

He landed at Lyme Regis on 11 June, recruiting 3,000 volunteers on his arrival. He marched to Somerset, was crowned king in Chard and again in Taunton on 21 June, by which time his troops had swollen to 7,000. Onwards to Bridgwater, to a civic reception and another coronation at the Cornhill. In the days that followed, he travelled through Westonzoyland, Glastonbury, Pensford, had a skirmish near Bristol and another at Keynsham, where his troops came off somewhat the worse. A more successful skirmish took place at Norton St Philip, where the king's troops walked straight into an ambush. From there they marched to Frome, but the weather had turned. Despite the recent victory, morale was in decline and his rebel troops were drifting home. After two days' rest at Wells, he returned on 2 July to Bridgwater, where he knew the local men showed greater commitment to his cause.

Monmouth had now heard the news of Argyle's defeat in Scotland. No longer would the king's forces be divided. Monmouth needed to act fast. Lord Feversham, with his Royalist troops, had by now arrived and was camped at Westonzoyland, with 2,000 foot and 700 horse. The camp had the benefit of the Bussex Rhyne (a deep wide ditch) on two sides and a line of cannon on the other, making it difficult to attack.

Whilst camped there, one of the king's officers, with dishonourable intentions, visited the home of a Westonzoyland lady. It proved to be his downfall. Twelve-year-old Mary Bridge, the lady's daughter, realising her mother's dilemma, killed the officer with his own sword. The girl was arrested and taken to Feversham, who released her and gifted her, as a souvenir, the officer's sword, which was subsequently put into the care of the Blake Museum.

A scene from the 1927 Pageant depicting Monmouth being honoured as king in Bridgwater.

(FROM THE ROGER EVANS COLLECTION)

The Battle of Sedgemoor memorial at Westonzoyland.

(FROM ROGER EVANS COLLECTION)

Meanwhile, a Chedzoy man, loyal to Monmouth, had gone to the tower of Chedzoy Church and recorded the information regarding the strength and position of the Royalist encampment. He was able to report to Monmouth that the king's troops had been drinking, were relaxed and expecting Monmouth to head north. Monmouth went to the top of the tower of St Mary's Church and looked across towards Westonzoyland with the aid of a telescope. He knew that his best opportunity was a surprise night attack. He was down to just 6,000 men and needed to act before more drifted away. He was also aware of the ability of the king's troops. He had served with many of them.

At 11 o'clock on the evening of 5 July 1685 Monmouth led his troops out of Bridgwater and along the Bath Road. They marched past Sydenham Manor into Bradney Lane and on to Peasey Farm, where the heavy equipment was left ready for collection after the battle. Through the darkness, Richard Godfrey, a local man, led them across the moor, over the Black Ditch and across Langmoor Rhyne, silently approaching the encampment of the king's troops. With just the Bussex Rhyne to cross, Captain Hucker accidentally fired his musket and the alarm was raised. The initial attack which followed was successful, but was eventually repelled when the Royalists turned their guns on their attackers. An unsuccessful cavalry charge from the rebels ended in a chaotic retreat, spreading panic through the untrained troops. From there on, the outcome was inevitable.

Artillery fire, followed by cavalry charges, resulted in hundreds lying dead on the fields of Sedgemoor. Monmouth escaped, only to be caught some days later disguised as a woman. He was later

executed in the Tower of London. Back on the battlefield, the slaughter continued. Rebels were mercilessly hunted down, their bodies left hanging from trees along the Bridgwater to Glastonbury road. In all, 500 rebels were locked up in Westonzoyland church, 22 being hanged on the way and five dying in the church, while 19 from that group were hanged the following day. The routing continued as troopers rode through the fields, tracking down hidden rebels. Many were shot for sport, like hares being flushed out for the guns.

The battle over, Feversham was recalled to London and replaced by Colonel Percy Kirke, who had a special role to play. The king had ordered Judge Jeffreys to conduct the trials of the rebels, trials which were to become known as the Bloody Assizes. These, he was told, were to be wrapped up in days, rather than months, leaving no opportunity for another rebellion to simmer beneath the surface. Despite stories to the contrary, Jeffreys never came to Bridgwater. He presided elsewhere, at Exeter, Dorchester, Taunton and Wells. What he did, however, was to instruct Kirke to soften up the rebels so that all pleaded guilty even if they were not. Kirke's technique was to invite the rebels to plead either innocent or guilty. Those who pleaded innocent were immediately taken outside and hanged. This doubtless acted as a great incentive to the others to plead guilty.

During this period Kirke lodged at Marycourt, a building now called the Carnival Inn, so that he could watch the hangings on the Cornhill. One of those due for execution was Roger Hoar who, having been sentenced to death, was taken to the Cornhill but reprieved just in time when his family delivered the deeds to his property. Two years later he was mayor of Bridgwater and now lies buried in St Mary's churchyard. Hundreds were executed and over 2,000 deported, all the Bridgwater men going to Barbados except for one, who was sent to Jamaica. Whilst this may sound an idyllic posting, it must be remembered that this was the seventeenth century and that those deported would have been crammed in the sweaty holds of small sailing ships for weeks on end. Those who survived the journey were then put to work in sweltering conditions as slaves, receiving the same cruel treatment as their negro counterparts.

The following month, King James II visited the town. The local civic leaders must have been in continuous fear as to what might befall them, having been party to Monmouth's coronation. In the wake of the rebellion, Bridgwater was declared a 'rebel town'. Without doubt, the town's religious loyalties still leaned towards Protestant Nonconformism and in 1692 the Baptist Chapel was built on its present-day site. This was replaced in 1835. In the seventeenth century, the local Puritans used the Baptist's pulpit for their services and were imprisoned for so doing under the Act of Uniformity.

Somerset Trade Tokens

So unsettled had been the seventeenth century that confidence in the coin of the realm was at a low ebb. During Saxon times a penny weighed 24 grams. By the time of Queen Elizabeth I, pennies had shrunk to the point where they were hard to spot in the bottom of one's purse. The copper-based farthings that were introduced were unpopular. Traders found it necessary to introduce their own currency, trade tokens. Early versions were of silver but latterly they were made of brass. Unacceptable as common currency, they could only be exchanged at the store of the producer, or perhaps one or two other stores where arrangements for their exchange existed. Officially they were illegal but it would have been impractical to take them out of circulation.

From 1649 until 1672, when Charles II introduced a new range of coins, these trade tokens abounded albeit with limited circulation covering just two or three streets where they could be traded. Bridgwater even had its own farthing, coined in 1666, with the town coat of arms on one side and a five-arched bridge on the other. Variations existed with six arches and with and without flags flying. Those local traders who produced tokens are shown in the table below.

Between 1787 and 1817, trade tokens made a return due to the scarcity of copper and the proliferation of forged coins. Bridgwater introduced its own halfpenny with the motto 'For change not fraud', with the coat of arms of the castle and three-arched bridge. It was issued by 'Holloway & Son and Post Office' and was inscribed on the reverse side with 'On demand we pay ½d'.

A further resurgence of local coins came in the late-nineteenth century, when coins were used mostly for pub games and hence were issued by the many public houses – the Alexander Hotel in St Mary Street; the Bath Bridge Inn; the Beaufort Arms; the Bristol Arms Hotel in the High Street; the British Flag; the Cross Rifles; the Crown Inn; the First and Last; the Devonshire Arms in Eastover; the Hope Inn; the Lions Club; the Three Crowns Inn; the White Hart Hotel. Many of these tokens were in use until the Second World War.

TRADERS' TOKENS

Alexander Atkins, 1654

John Crapp, 1659 and 1670

Edward Dawes Brasier, 1657

John Hunt, 1651

William Page, 1669

Edward Pettitt, 1654

James Safforde, 1658

William Sealey, 1652 and 1654

John Rogers, 1669, an erect sword between wings with the town's High Cross on the reverse

John Bone, 1656, depicting a hand-held wool comb

Joseph Franklin, 1666, depicting a wool comb

William Goodridge, 1669, depicting a ship

Robert Haviland, 1652, showing a merchant's mark

John Linton, 1656–69, The Salter's Arms

John Palmer, 1664, The Draper's Arms

Christopher Roberts, covered cup

William Serlland, 1654

Barges at the Langport slipway, c.1905.

(FROM THE ROGER EVANS COLLECTION)

CHAPTER 5

The River and Shipping

Earliest Records

We can date shipping in Bridgwater back to at least AD1200, when William Brewer was granted the rights to collect lastage, a tax on cargoes. In 1233 the constable of Bridgwater was ordered to assist the abbots and monks of Tewkesbury in shipping timber and lead from Bridgwater for the repair of their church.

In 1277, the Patent Rolls record sailors of Bridgwater being summoned to assist Edward I in his Welsh campaign. Perhaps Bridgwater men were being asked once too often, for in 1302 Edward I ordered Thomas de Werbelton and Peter de Donewyco to punish, at their discretion, the people of Bridgwater who had promised to send a well-armed ship to help in the war against the Scots and which had thus far failed to turn up. It appears, however, that it did not pay to upset the Bridgwater sailors, for by November of that year the tone had changed. Peter de Donewyco was instructed to work with the Sheriff of Somerset to see if the bailiffs and men of Bridgwater could be 'persuaded' to join the expedition against the Scots.

In 1300 Simon de Montacute owned two galleys and a barge at Bridgwater. In 1306, the *Sauneye*, mastered by William de Wyght of Bridgwater, carried lead to Gascony.

The following year corn and victuals were carried to Gascony but, with those exceptions, nothing was allowed to leave the country. In 1311 Thomas Kirkeby was ordered to superintend the provisioning, with supplies for seven weeks, of a Bridgwater ship to join the fight against Robert the Bruce. However, a condition of the order was that the provision of such a ship was not to be to the prejudice of Kirkeby's trade nor was it to be seen as a precedent. This clearly reflects the power and influence that the port of Bridgwater traders had in that period.

In 1314, 1317 and 1322 Bridgwater supplied further ships for the Scottish wars, the latter of these being for the transport of soldiers from Ireland to Scotland. Also in 1317, John Godwin, a Bridgwater merchant, is recorded as importing wine from Bordeaux. On his arrival in Bordeaux, some French merchants chartered the ship to go to Rouen but it seems Godwin had been hoodwinked for, on his arrival, his ship was seized by the Duke of Brittany. It required the intervention of the king to sort the matter out.

Defending the Nation

It appears that trouble was brewing between the two nations and in 1328 an order was sent through the mayor and bailiffs of Bridgwater that all ship owners should prepare to repel an attack from the French. In 1330 a number of Bridgwater ships were involved when the king ordered a small fleet to collect at Bridgwater, ready to take on the French. Bridgwater, clearly significant as a port and as a shipbuilding centre, by 1348 had been officially classified as a port. For the next 20 years England lost its naval supremacy to the French and, in 1375 alone, 39 ships were taken in Bourneuf Bay, including Bridgwater's *Saint Marie*, a vessel of 170 tons valued at £180. Ten years later, in 1385, a 120-ton Bridgwater ship joined the fleet of the Duke of Lancaster in an attempt to obtain possession of the Kingdom of Castile.

Bridgwater ships were regularly being used to transfer troops and provisions for the war, and likewise were ordered not to supply the enemy. In similar fashion, Bridgwater ships and merchants were not allowed to trade with the Irish, since we were also at war with them. It seems that John of Godesland, who was trading out of Bridgwater, was determined to break this embargo. Two Bridgwater bailiffs, Richard Dyer and Roger Wolanton, arrested an Irish ship which Godesland had loaded with provisions. It appears that they actually swam out to the ship to achieve this – a particularly brave effort. Godesland threatened the two bailiffs with violence and they in turn reported the matter to the king, who instructed the sheriff to take Godesland to Westminster. Eight years later, the same two brave bailiffs were fined £86.5s.4d. for allowing a cargo of that value to escape them. They were eventually let off the fine when it was revealed that they had, in fact, arrested the offending vessel, which had then escaped by force of arms, John Godesland once again being the perpetrator of the deed.

Wheat, beans and pulses, bacon pigs and other agricultural produce moved through the port in considerable quantities. Much of this was exported to France, Spain and Ireland by such traders as David le Palmer, John Cole and John Michel. Much of the shipping in the fourteenth century was in wine and in 1396 an extra-strong wooden gangway was constructed to help with the unloading of the huge wine containers. In 1360 Adam Beste received two tuns (a tun is 216 gallons) from Dunwich on the Suffolk coast.

Imports in the fourteenth century included wine from Bordeaux and herring from the Channel. Later imports included timber, twine, hemp, linseed, esparto grass, hides and valonia, the latter item being produced from acorns and used as a dye in tanning. By 1488 the trade in wool and cloth had increased so much that a new slipway was built, using stone from Pidsbury, to handle the traffic to Langport.

From the 1450s there are records of the continuous repairs associated with maintaining a busy quayside. There were new slings, hawsers and pulleys for the crane, along with tallow to grease the pulleys and tar to preserve the timbers. The bushels used to measure salt and dry goods were regularly replaced and workmen endured the never-ending task of clearing the silt which accumulated on the slipways.

By the 1480s, around 1,000 rolls of cloth per year were being exported. By the sixteenth century exports included the serges and in later centuries timber, pit props, cement, plaster of Paris, gypsum, and bricks, tiles and pipes from the clay works of more recent times, by which time coal and timber dominated the imports.

Smuggling and Piracy

The earliest records we have of the evasion of customs duty is from the Borough Court records of April 1380, when John Cole, a merchant of the town, was found to have:

> ... held back and concealed by his trickery and subtlety the lord's customs of corn sold to foreign merchants in the harbour of Bridgwater during 12 years, to wit, 10,000 quarters of corn, in deception of lord and lordship of Bridgwater reaching the sum of £20. And that J.C. in the same manner for the whole time aforesaid withdrew the customs of the lord and lordship of iron, fish, salt, wine and other merchandise sold to divers foreign merchants.

Shortly afterwards, there was another court case concerning yet more individuals who would deprive the lord of his duties. In this case the miscreants had persuaded a ship from Ilfracombe to dock at Combwich, where they could unload its cargo of herring. They did the same with a ship from Tenby, a Cornish vessel and a barge, which were laden with salt and corn. The villains were found guilty with damages of £100. What is particularly of interest is not just that two of the group were Bridgwater burgesses, but that the third member of this band of smugglers was the vicar of Otterhampton!

In 1410 John Kedwelly sent a formal complaint to Parliament concerning his loss of a boat, the *Cog John*, at Harfleur, in France. Frenchmen had seized it along with the crew and cargo, demanding a ransom for their release. At St Malo he had lost another ship, stolen and sold to the Spanish. These were dangerous days but the profit from such trade made the risks worthwhile.

An interesting case is recorded in the borough archives of 1458. William Founs, a Bridgwater merchant, had travelled to Bilbao, where he agreed the purchase of nine tuns of wine from the Spaniard John de Vessy. There was an agreement that if the ship was plundered during its trip to Bridgwater by English privateers, then Founs would suffer the loss, but if the perpetrators were of any other nationality, then de Vessy would take the financial hit. The cargo was lost, and not at English hands, but de Vessy argued to the contrary. Meanwhile, Founs had gone to Bilbao with a cargo including 16 wool cloths. These he placed in the safe keeping of a Spaniard by the name of Perrons, who was in league with de Vessy and kept the cloths as payment for his Spanish colleague. Founs took the matter to the Spanish court which, instead of providing Founs with the justice he sought, threw him in gaol for not settling what they claimed he owed to de Vessy. Founs complained to the Lord Chancellor and the Sheriff of Somerset, who issued a warrant for de Vessy's arrest should he ever visit England. He did, and was promptly placed in prison, along with two of his Spanish colleagues, for not releasing Founs's cargo of cloth. And there we must leave them – the Bridgwater man in a Spanish gaol and the Spaniard in a Bridgwater gaol – since I have no idea how the story finishes.

In the early decades of the sixteenth century, the shipping trade went into decline and, by 1550, was at half its former strength. This raises questions as to whether the trade had actually dropped or was simply not being recorded. In 1565 a special commission recorded that:

> Bridgwater is much frequented and haunted with traffic of merchants and merchandises to the inward and outward and it is to be continued for that purpose. There are no places or sellers, warehouses or store houses near unto the said port where lading or unloading is or hath been used whereby the Queen's Majesty is defrauded of her customs as far as we know.

This would suggest that little or no smuggling was going on. Five years later, the Bridgwater ship *Jhesus*, owned by John Boyce, was recorded as available for duty in His Majesty's Navy with the following Bridgwater men on board: James Dockett, Richard Cogen, Rupert Stephens, Richard Hardricke, George Hoe, Robert Mayo, William Cooke, Thomas Phillips and John Prewett.

It would appear that the town in general was in decline during this period. When John Leland visited in 1540, he recorded that some 200 homes were in a state of ruin, and a quarter of a century later the population had shrunk to pre-1440 levels. With this decline, the focus of attention moved away from the castle and the borough in general and towards the port and the ship owners and traders became the most influential members of the community. Undoubtedly, periods of conflict with the French and Spanish made trade difficult. The need to trade effectively with the continent is borne out by the actions of Mr Boyes, the mayor, and Messrs Newport, Watkyns & Moleyns, who were among the Bridgwater traders who donated swords, daggers, armour, poleaxes, bows and arrows and various other items to help regain control of the port of Calais. In 1569, the town supplied billmen, pikemen, gunners and archers, as well as armour and various weapons to help fight the Spanish.

By 1592 the number of ships registered at Bridgwater had declined to seven, ranging from 10 tons to 30 tons. By the end of 1596 there was just one barque recorded. Undoubtedly, in the post-Armada period, trade had dried up. The sixteenth century had ended in depression for Bridgwater and the century to follow offered further difficult times. The town had to wait for 100 years before trade really picked up again.

Various periods of conflict in the seventeenth century resulted in the levying of high excise duty to fund the conflicts. Inevitably this led to smuggling. Bridgwater, as a port, had responsibility for collecting duty on most types of imports, even as far along the coast as Minehead. The duty officer had considerable distances to travel and, needless to say, when his back was turned, there were those who would take advantage. Duty officer Daniel Yates complained that the ship *Encrease*, from Virginia, in June 1679 landed 60 hogsheads of tobacco before he had chance to collect the duty, which he managed to do on the remaining 125 hogsheads. Duty could only be collected if he had witnessed the unloading. George Atwell once reported that a wagonload of cloth, so big that it took 12 oxen to pull it, had escaped his attention.

The government sent in two investigators, William Culliford and Arnold Browne. Between them they gained confessions to 101 tuns of wine and brandy and 2,357 packages of linen having escaped duty over a three-year period. A search of the town turned up contraband all over the place. In their final report they referred to the custom's collector as drunken, dishonest and seldom if ever sober!

The Voyage of the *Emanuel*

Frobisher's 1578 voyage to discover the Northwest passage to China is well documented. One of the 15 ships on that expedition was Bridgwater's *Emanuel* which, as a deep-sea fishing vessel or small trader, was built for the heavy seas. On this classic voyage, the fleet met a violent storm during which the *Emanuel* became separated from the rest of the fleet. During that time, the crew discovered a previously unknown island, which they charted and named the Land of Busse. For years afterwards the island appeared on maritime charts but was never encountered again. Presumably it was a huge iceberg.

Blossoming Trade

With the turmoil of the seventeenth century consigned to history, Bridgwater's trade began to grow. Roger Hoar, who came close to being hanged, drawn and quartered after the Monmouth Rebellion, lost four ships in less than two years, one captured at Milford Haven by a French privateer. Wars with France made the Bridgwater merchants look closer to home for their maritime trade, and to Wales and Ireland in particular. William Alloway's main trade was in wool and tallow from Ireland, rock salt from Liverpool and tobacco from the West Indies. In 1697 John Trott built the *Friendship* for Alloway, whose ship the *Unity* is recorded as having taken more than 600 barrels of herring to Barbados in a single voyage.

Piracy did not always act against the interests of Bridgwater seafarers. In 1740, Philip Baker, a Bridgwater merchant, was granted permission for his ship the *Diana* to act as a privateer. This basically meant she was permitted to capture French ships for profit. The *Diana* was eventually captured herself by the French off the coast of Newfoundland.

By the mid-eighteenth century, coastal trade remained the greater part of the activity with beer, cider, meats, cheeses and bricks being shipped in and corn as the main outgoing commodity. Exports from the eighteenth century onwards included timber, pit wood, cement, plaster of Paris, gypsum, bricks, tiles and pipes, with coal and timber as the main imports. At the end of the eighteenth century, Bridgwater could boast 32 ships of her own, the bulk of the trade being in coal and timber.

Shipbuilding

During the eighteenth century, Bridgwater shipyards were producing ships at the rate of one per year. As early as 1593, Bridgwater had a shipwright. John Trott, who built the *Friendship* for John Alloway, had a dry dock and repair dock built on the East Quay. In 1671 the Admiralty had recognised Bridgwater as an approved centre for ship manufacture. The first really big ship was the brigantine *Nancy*, built in 1766.

In 1810, the year in which there was a failed attempt to build a canal from Combwich to Bridgwater, Carver's Yard on the East Quay was building ships of 200 tons, whilst Gough & Nation at Crowpill produced ships up to 350 tons. Between 1800 and 1850, seven shipyards produced 51 vessels. In the next 50 years, a further 88 were produced, mostly sloops and schooners. Although the river could take these large ships, most of the vessels were humbler affairs, around 60–70 tons capacity. As demand for ships built of metal rather than timber increased, so the Bridgwater shipyards declined. Gough's was closed around 1880, leaving just the yard of Francis James Carver & Sons. It was from their yard in 1894 that the 95ft ketch *Kate and Annie* was christened by Miss Ada Carver as she smashed a bottle of wine over the stern. It was from the same yard that the *Irene*, the last Bridgwater-built ketch, was launched in May 1907, built for Colthurst & Symonds and designed to work the channel ports.

The last vessel to enter Carver's Yard was the *Crowpill*, captained by the popular Jibo Searles. He had a reputation as the only man who could navigate the tortuous River Parrett, even in the densest fog – yet he would rarely venture past Dunball if it seemed unlikely that he would dock at Bridgwater before the pubs closed. Carver's Yard closed but remained as a water-filled well until a tragic drowning in 1959 resulted in it being filled in the following year.

One of the larger ships launched in the town was the *Brittania* in September 1831. The Bridgwater *Alfred* described the event as follows:

At an early hour the quays and banks of the river presented an interesting sight. All the vessels in the harbour were decorated with their colours and the banks were lined with crowds of people of all ages and conditions mingled in one close mass, presenting to the eye a living scene of interesting variety. Precisely at eight o'clock, the sound of the hammer striking away the blocks was heard and immediately the majestic fabric glided into the water, amidst the deafening cheers of the surrounding thousands. We never saw a finer launch and not the slightest accident occurred. To the bulk of the spectators, the launching of a ship is nothing more than a pageant, a spectacle

The Irene *at Bristol's Festival of the Seas, 1996.*
(FROM THE ROGER EVANS COLLECTION)

which they rush on to enjoy without any knowledge of, or even any desire of knowing, the means by which the operation is performed.

In 1857, the *Admiral Blake* was built at John Gough's yard, being a ship of 190 tons and 100ft in length.

Petrel, *the paddle-tug at Carver's Yard, built in 1863.* (FROM THE ROGER EVANS COLLECTION)

The Crowpill *in Bridgwater Dock, c.1950.*   (FROM THE ROGER EVANS COLLECTION)

Larger still was the *Cesarea*, a 400-ton barque built at the same yard in 1864.

At least 167 ships were built and registered in the town, sloops and schooners for the coastal traffic, ketches and square riggers for the deep sea voyages. Bridgwater smacks were built with full and deep lines, with a straight stem and square sterns. Until 1908, Quantock oak was used. Around this shipping and shipbuilding activity there sprang up all the associated trades: rope makers in the area we now know as Rope Walk and another halfway along Chilton Street; ships' chandlers (one being on the corner of East Quay and Eastover); sail makers, not to mention all the inns required to serve the needs of the marine community. Bridgwater was left with a legacy of pub names which reflected its maritime

Waddon's Rope Walk in Eastover, 1865. The premises were destroyed by fire in 1951.
(FROM THE BRIDGWATER TOWN COUNCIL COLLECTION, COURTESY THE BLAKE MUSEUM)

The corner of Eastover and East Quay, with a ship's chandler (on the corner), *Mole the Chemist and Waddon's the ropemakers, c.1865.* (FROM THE BRIDGWATER TOWN COUNCIL COLLECTION, COURTESY THE BLAKE MUSEUM)

Crowpill House on the West Quay, c.1865. The home of the Sully family, shippers and coal merchants, this was later used as a youth hostel. American troops were entertained here during the Second World War.
(FROM THE BRIDGWATER TOWN COUNCIL COLLECTION, COURTESY THE BLAKE MUSEUM)

Ox roast on the River Parrett, 1895. (FROM THE ROGER EVANS COLLECTION)

Saltlands, 1895, when ships were locked by the ice.
(FROM THE BRIDGWATER TOWN COUNCIL COLLECTION, COURTESY THE BLAKE MUSEUM)

past, albeit many of them now closed: the Ship Afloat, the Ship Aground, the Dolphin, the Hope & Anchor, the British Flag, the Crowpill Inn, the Steam Packet Inn, the Sailor's Return, the Sailor's Home, the Salmon Inn (now the River Parrett Inn), the Shipwright's Arms, the Mariner's Arms and the Boat & Anchor. And in St John Street there was once the Mariners' Chapel, built in 1837 for those of a more sober nature. It was capable of seating 350 people and survived until the 1960s.

Such was the volume of trade that Bridgwater had a Vice Consul for Germany (George Bryant Sully) and another for Scandinavia, plus a customs house, all based on the West Quay. Excise matters were dealt with at the Lamb Inn, now known as the Duke. Through the nineteenth century, the shipping trade was dominated by four companies:

(a) Havilland, whose small vessels traded in coal, culm and limestone.

(b) Axford, whose faster schooners were used for coastal trading

(c) Stuckey & Bagehot, whose larger ships had to wait for the opening of the docks before they ventured past Combwich, and

(d) Sully, perhaps the best remembered name, trading in coal and culm around the UK and France.

By 1851 at least 200 people were employed as mariners (my great-great-grandfather amongst them), pilots or seamen, plus nearly 30 more in ship-building. It was, of course, the building of a bridge across the River Parrett which, centuries earlier, had created the port of Bridgwater. Whilst the big ships, many of them coal-carrying trows, moored up on the seaward side of the bridge, flat-bottomed barges and lighters, capable of riding the bore, moored up on the landward side, waiting to take goods on to Langport and Taunton. The barges of the Colthurst & Symonds brickyards were a regular sight at the Langport slipway. The lighters had the advantage of being able to pass under the bridge and collect their cargo direct from the larger ships.

The Dangers of the Bore

The twice-daily tidal wave which pushes up the River Parrett, known as the bore, is usually an innocuous affair attracting little or no attention as it travels at about 6 miles per hour. However, on the spring tides and when the wind is in the right direction, its impact can have greater significance. In 1875, the tidal bore stood at 10ft high, sufficient to flood most of low-lying Somerset. Bores of 1–2ft are much more the norm but even these can catch the unprepared by surprise. The *Caerleon* broke away from her moorings near the Town Bridge and became jammed under the bridge as the tide continued to rise. It seemed she was doomed to having her back broken, or simply being submerged,

until the tide eventually turned and she survived the ordeal.

Occasionally, and indeed frequently in earlier centuries, someone would drown in the river. Such is the strength of the tide that the victim's body can be washed up and down the river for days, normally unseen on the riverbed, until the corpse inflates with the gases of decomposition and, several weeks after the fatality, rises to the surface. Typically, a body lost at Bridgwater will surface at Dunball a month or so later.

Whilst the river can be dangerous at any time, it is probably at its safest at full tide, as the tide begins to turn. It is then that the river is deepest and almost still. I am sure it must have been at such times that Sam Scott, an American diver, performed his stunts. On at least two separate occasions, he dived the 70ft from the foretop gallant-yard of the *John and Mary* into the river. The *Bridgwater Mercury* reported both occasions, declaring, 'He'll do it once too often.'

It's a cruel river but it has been tamed on at least one occasion. The big freeze of 1895 saw the Parrett frozen solid from bank to bank; a bonfire and ox roast was organised on the river, as had happened before, in 1881.

At its peak, ships lined the two quays of Bridgwater, often double-parking. It is told that my great-great-grandfather, James Thorne, a Bridgwater mariner, once walked from the East Quay to the West Quay across the decks of the ships moored near the Town Bridge. Many of these ships had to be manoeuvred into place, which was the job of the hobblers, a tough breed of men who, walking the river banks, would haul the ships along the river to their place of mooring. The work was not only hard but competitive. The hobblers would race down to Combwich or Dunball in order to be the first to take the ropes from an incoming ship.

The Docks

With a 30ft tidal rise and fall and limited space along the quayside, the advantages of having a dock with a constant water-level became clear. This was in 1840, when the dock as we see it today was built. From 1811 to 1840 canal schemes were popping up all over the country. In 1820 the Bridgwater to Taunton Canal scheme was proposed mainly to combat the problems of the river silting up to such an extent that it became impassable at its higher reaches after long dry spells. In 1827 the canal was opened from Taunton to Huntworth, where it linked to the river. This created a price war between the Tone Navigators and the canal owners which did neither side any good and resulted in numerous court cases over a period of five years. In the end, the dispute was only resolved when the canal company bought out its competitors. In 1837 Royal Assent was granted to extend the canal to Bridgwater and to build a dock.

Double-parking along the quays, c.1907.   (FROM THE ROGER EVANS COLLECTION)

The engineer in charge was Thomas Maddicks, of Devon. A total of 105,000 cu ft of clay was dug out by a workforce of hundreds of navvies. The clay was used for brick making or thrown up on a giant spoil heap, which was to become known as the Mump and which has since been removed to permit housing development. There was only one fatality in its construction, caused when a wagon carrying a 6-ton stone from Puriton ran out of control in a thunderstorm. One major feat of engineering was the creation of the cut where the canal passed through the area from Albert Street to Victoria Road, the passageway carved through the red sandstone earning itself the name of The Canyon. Sadly, Thomas Maddicks died in the poorhouse in Taunton aged 84.

By 1838 the Grand Western Canal had been linked to the Bridgwater to Taunton canal at the Taunton end. This meant that once the canal was open all the way to Bridgwater it was possible to travel from Bridgwater to Tiverton by canal.

The dock finally opened in 1841 and on 25 March, the Bridgwater-built sloop the *Henry* glided through the lock-gates with Captain Giles Billing at the helm,

towed by the port's first steam tug, the *Endeavour*, which had sailed down the river to meet her, complete with a band providing music for the many dignitaries on board. Thousands of locals lined the docksides, the day having been declared a Bank Holiday. Cannons fired and church bells rang, the national anthem was sung and both the George Hotel and the Royal Clarence, providing celebratory dinners, were filled to capacity. From that day on, ships of up to 180ft in length and 31ft across could enter the safety of the dock.

At the quayside, the infrastructure of the docks had already begun to appear. Wares Warehouse was built in three phases. The three bays at the canal end were bonded warehouses for the canal company. The rest was added for the Bristol & Exeter Railway Co. (later part of the Great Western). Diagonally opposite, across the dock, was Bowering's animal feed mill, which still stands alongside the Newtown Lock, which provides the link to the canal. To add to the infrastructure, a link was also required to the Bristol to Exeter Railway, which reached the town for the first time in 1841. Such a link would require a railway bridge to be built across the river, which

The docks viewed from the Mump, c.1905.
(FROM THE ROGER EVANS COLLECTION)

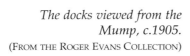

The docks viewed from the canal end, c.1904.

(FROM THE ROGER EVANS COLLECTION)

Just inside the dock can be seen the stern of the **Eroder** *with its water cannon, used to blast the clay deposits from the river bank, c.1904.*

(FROM THE ROGER EVANS COLLECTION)

The dredger Bertha, *c.1950.*   (FROM THE ROGER EVANS COLLECTION)

Left and below: *Quayside crane and bollard.*
(FROM THE ROGER EVANS COLLECTION)

Dock repairs (right), *which often required the services of a diver, c.1920* (above).

Robert Squibbs (in the top hat), *a local auctioneer and estate agent, c.1865.*
(FROM THE BRIDGWATER TOWN COUNCIL COLLECTION, COURTESY THE BLAKE MUSEUM)

The Steep Holm *was built to fit into Bridgwater dock – just.*
(FROM THE ROGER EVANS COLLECTION)

Brunel design, and over which traffic still goes today. Completing Brunel's contribution to the dock's infrastructure was the dredger *Bertha*. The main problem for the dock operators was the heavy silting from which it suffered. The steam-driven *Bertha* was designed to run up and down a chain from one end of the dock to the other. At the end of each journey the chain would be moved a bit further across the end of the dock, so that, over a period of several passes, the entire dock basin would be covered. The concept was simple. Imagine if the dock were drained and a bulldozer was used to push the silt deposit to one end of the dock. The bulldozer blade is down in one direction and up in the other. That was how Bertha worked, but under the water. She had a large vertical beam which could be raised and lowered. At the bottom end was a 'bulldozer' blade which shifted the mud down to the dock gates so that, when the river level was lower than the dock level, the gates could be opened and the mud flushed into the river. It was a never-ending challenge.

Following the opening of the docks, the number of tugs bringing in vessels increased at the same time as the number of hobblers declined, their role having become simply to help the ships moor to the dockside bollards. Other jobs were lost as man-powered cranes or derricks were replaced by their steam-driven equivalents. Perhaps the SS *Masuren* should have used the hobblers in 1928. A German timber boat, she hit the river bank at the turn of the tide. Lodged on the bank as the tide was dropping, she began to keel over. The only way the captain could save his ship was to cut loose the timber and let it fall into the river. For months thereafter, riverside homes boasted new garden sheds and chicken huts, with no one saying where the materials had come from.

Shortly after the opening of the docks, while most ships entered fairly easily, in late 1841 the *Eliza*, of Gloucester, managed to hit the bascule bridge through 'neglect of duty', causing considerable damage. Extensive repairs were required and the *Eliza* was embargoed and never entered the dock again.

The Latter Days

Ships continued to use both the East and West Quays until just before the Second World War. At its peak, Bridgwater saw 4,000 dockings a year, an average of 11 ships coming in on the tides each day, turning over as much as 250,000 tons of coal, timber and other products in 1861. That was the heyday of Bridgwater's shipping concerns, however, and we now consider its demise in the town. After a gap of 11 years, the steamer *Parrett* used the East Quay several times between 1947 and 1949 to offload flour. She was the last to use the quays.

The last sailing craft to use the quays was probably the *Trio*, owned by the Warren family of Kendale Road, in 1934. At the docks, in the years after the

York House, on the corner of Eastover and East Quay, was a grocer and provisions merchant supplying the ships.
(FROM THE BRIDGWATER TOWN COUNCIL COLLECTION, COURTESY THE BLAKE MUSEUM)

would prevent the tall-masted sailing ships from reaching the quaysides and the dock. To overcome this problem a steam-driven telescopic bridge, known today as the Black Bridge, was designed by Isambard Kingdom Brunel. In its working days it would telescope back onto the eastern side of the river. Opened in 1871, initially the only traffic over it was horse-drawn, and a similar horse-drawn railway link existed which ran down to Dunball.

The telescopic bridge was supported on two large piers, one each side of the river. When ships came up the river, a section of the rail track on the east side of the river would be slid sideways into an otherwise open space alongside the track. This then created a gap where the line had previously been into which a section of the bridge could be retracted, rolling on small wheels which can still be seen beneath the bridge. The whole was powered by a steam-driven engine, the greater part of which was destroyed by British Rail but which does survive in the care of the Westonzoyland Engine Trust.

Road traffic at the dock was facilitated by the building of a bascule bridge, again believed to be a

Timber-yard workers with the isolation hospital, formerly the workhouse, in the background.
(FROM THE ROGER EVANS COLLECTION)

Second World War, the *Parrett*, the *Enid* (skippered by Warpy May) and the *Crowpill* (skippered by Jibo Searle) were regular visitors, bringing coal for the domestic and commercial markets, especially for the local Cellophane plant.

The decline of the shipping industry and the docks dates back to the very time the dock was opened and a rail link established with South Wales, using the Severn Tunnel. Local river traffic went into steep decline between 1878 and 1900. The growth of the railways, steam replacing sail, ships getting larger, were all nails in the coffin. By 1907 the last commercial barge was making its journey along the canal to Taunton. At the end of its days, the only commodities passing through the dock were coal and timber. Bridgwater Dock ceased to be an active port in 1969, when the Courtauld's Cellophane factory switched its power plant from coal to heavy fuel oil.

The official Act of Parliament closing the dock came in 1971.

The canal had by that time fallen into ruin, although subsequent improvements have been made in recognition of its potential as a recreational facility. Likewise, the docks have been imaginatively developed into a marina, which has yet to achieve its full potential, and Bridgwater owes a debt of gratitude to the entrepreneur and businessman Colin Wilkins, whose vision it was to establish the marina.

Perhaps one day another vision will be realised if a barrage is placed across the river, maybe at Dunball, thus allowing open access from the river to the dock and creating a circular route of some 24 miles for canal and river cruising, up the canal to Taunton and back down the river, with links to King Sedgemoor Drain and the Huntspill River, creating the 'Somerset Broads'.

Bridgwater and Kilve Royal Mail, c.1910.

(FROM THE ROGER EVANS COLLECTION, COURTESY THE LATE MRS G. AUTHERS)

The Three Crowns Hotel in St Mary Street, c.1898. A campaign poster on the wall encouraged men to defend their rights to Sunday opening.

(FROM THE BRIDGWATER TOWN COUNCIL COLLECTION, COURTESY THE BLAKE MUSEUM)

CHAPTER 6

Eighteenth-Century Bridgwater

Law and Order

A measure of the growth of Bridgwater can be estimated from the number of constables employed within the borough – a total of 17 in the early part of the eighteenth century. Their role was different from that of the constables of today, and more specialised. There were two each for bread weighing, market surveying, shambles wardening, sealing and proving leather and ale tasting; three each for salt weighing and examining hides and skins, and just one for herring packing. By the end of the century these positions had been consolidated, first down to five officers and then to three, but by then two street constables and two watchmen had been introduced. So many constables at the beginning of the century may seem somewhat excessive in a population of around 2,200, a figure which puts into perspective the seriousness of the plague epidemic which hit the town in 1711 and during which there were five deaths in a single day. A further epidemic, in which large numbers of children died, hit the town in 1729–30.

It was to Bridgwater that many people were brought for trial in the case of serious offences. In 1730 Jack White was sentenced to death at the Bridgwater Assizes for the murder of Robert Sutton in South Somerset. John Walford was sentenced to death in 1789 for the murder of his wife in a case which has left as its legacy 'Dead Woman's Ditch' and 'Walford's Gibbet' on the Quantocks. These were just two of the many death sentences imposed in the town. One case which we may find surprisingly harsh today is that of Sarah Crocker, who was sentenced to death at the town's assizes for stealing the sacramental plate from Butcombe Church.

Stagecoach Travel

Until the railway arrived in Bridgwater, in 1841, the only way to travel, other than by river, was to walk, ride or take a horse-drawn carriage. The eighteenth century was the age of coach travel, the coaching inns which served those travellers and the wagoners with their teams of horses. Coaches, which travelled at around 5 miles an hour, were typically pulled by teams of four to six horses, which also had to be cared for. In the skittle alley of the Three Crowns in St Mary Street, now closed, metal rings attached to the alley wall indicated that it had once acted as a stable for coach horses. Most travel was during daylight hours and, since the journey to London could take three or four days, plenty of watering-holes were needed along the route, especially as the state of the roads was so bad. Indeed, so bad were the roads that one Bridgwater coach proprietor made it a rule never to employ any coachman who had not had his coach turn over, on the assumption that those who had would know how to right it again. By the mid-1800s, speeds had increased to 11 miles per hour and London could be reached in a day. The Swiftsure coach was one of those London Flyers which stopped at the Piper's Inn, Glastonbury, Wells, Shepton Mallet, Frome and Andover on its way to the capital.

Giles & Hooper Waggons travelled to London, leaving on Tuesday and Friday evenings and arriving a day later. Brown & Brice Waggons (daily from the Rose and Crown) and Whitmarsh Waggons (Monday, Wednesday and Saturday) also offered services to London. Snell's covered the Bristol to Exeter trips on alternate days, their pick-up point being the Ship Afloat in Market Street (Tuesday, Thursday and Saturday). Chadwell's Waggons set out from George Street while the Rose and Crown in St Mary Street was used by both Brown & Brice and Martin's Waggons, the latter working between Bath and Taunton.

The Three Crowns in St Mary Street served Webber's Waggons, which travelled to Honiton. Other local coach companies were Nation's Waggons (Bristol to Minehead), Granfield's Wagons (Bath to Minehead), Slocombe's (Bath to Stogumber) and Lavin's (Bristol to Wiveliscombe, up on Wednesday and down on Saturday).

The London coach used to leave from the East Quay outside the old Post Office, a building which still boasts a clock high up on its wall. The presence of the clock was important since, before the introduction of the railways, times varied across the country. Midday was when the sun was directly overhead, wherever you happened to be. Since London is to the east of Bridgwater by three degrees, midday was 12 minutes earlier than in Bridgwater, and so travellers would have to adjust their watches at each end of their journey. Hence it was important to keep an accurate clock, which was one of the roles of the postmaster, Mr Holloway. Whilst he may have kept an accurate clock, he still managed to get dismissed for daily blunders, including reading the London newspapers which had been paid for by the local business community. Worse, his customers had to wait until he had finished reading the latest copy. He was not the only postmaster to receive complaints. One of his

The staff of the Post Office on the East Quay, 1865. The man in the centre with the beard was Mr Lockyer, while his very tall colleague was Mr Dell.

(FROM THE BRIDGWATER TOWN COUNCIL COLLECTION, COURTESY THE BLAKE MUSEUM)

Postmen at the High Street office in 1904, prior to its move to the Cornhill.

(FROM THE BRIDGWATER TOWN COUNCIL COLLECTION, COURTESY THE BLAKE MUSEUM)

The old iron bridge in 1865. It was replaced in 1883.

(FROM THE BRIDGWATER TOWN COUNCIL COLLECTION, COURTESY THE BLAKE MUSEUM)

predecessors in 1675 was criticised for delivering the mail incorrectly – he could neither read nor write.

The St Mary Street Riots

The Swan Inn in Bridgwater was famous across the West Country as a hostelry. Based on the Cornhill, on the St Mary Street side, it had its origins in the early-seventeenth century and survived until around 1800. As with any town centre hostelry, there was the occasional violent incident, but few so notable as the one which took place on an otherwise quiet but hot Sunday evening in July 1717.

A troop of dragoons travelling from Bristol to Exeter had camped just outside the town and a group of their officers were drinking in the Swan. The session continued until the early hours of the morning, when Thomas Dowsett, William Freeman and Jonathan Cockram decided to call it a day. As they left, one of them was spotted taking a bag of someone else's money. The landlord was notified and he requested the return of the bag. Ensign Dowsett took offence, an argument ensued and Dowsett fired his pistol at the man who had reported the theft to the landlord, narrowly missing the man's head as the bullet lodged in the wall.

The mayor was summoned and he called out the town's two bailiffs. Outnumbered by the dragoons, they called out the part-time constables – an iron-monger and a maltster. A warrant for the arrest of the dragoon was issued and the soldiers closed ranks, drew their swords and sounded the call to arms on a drum. In next to no time, 40 or more dragoons responded to the call and the culprits escaped into St Mary Street, where the Riot Act was read. The

incident only came to a satisfactory conclusion when the dragoons' commanding officer arrived with an even larger force. The errant dragoons later appeared before the magistrates at Taunton.

Another unusual incident took place some years later, in 1739, when the Revd George Whitfield, an outspoken Nonconformist, was preaching in the open air at the invitation of the parish vicar. The content of the sermon was sufficiently controversial that the town's fire brigade were called out to put the hoses on him.

The Iron Bridge and the Turnpike Trusts

With the increase in travel, there was a need for the relatively narrow stone-built Town Bridge to be replaced with one more suited to stagecoaches rather than packhorses. In addition, the three stone arches acted as a barrier, holding back the water and creating problems in time of flood. Barges going under the bridge often became stuck as the tide rose and cargoes were swamped. It was decided that an iron bridge was required, the emphasis being on a high arch, copying the one built at Coalbrookdale by Abraham Darby.

The various parts were cast at Ironbridge in 1795 and from there were floated down the River Severn on rafts and up the River Parrett to Bridgwater. The completed bridge, which formed an elliptical arch, was opened in 1797. Robert Codrington of Ivy House in Friarn Street was mayor at the time and it was his initials which were put on the commemorative plaque which adorned the bridge, and which now adorns the portico of the Royal Clarence building.

(FROM THE ROGER EVANS COLLECTION)

View with fishermen's boats along Salmon Parade towards the old iron bridge, 1865.

Clockwise from top left: *Turnpike roads and toll-houses at Salmon Lane; at Monmouth Street looking into Bristol Road; at Taunton Road, where the toll-house can still be seen opposite the Hope Inn (the inn is not pictured here); at the top of Durleigh Hill; and at Wembdon Road, where the toll-house also survives.*

(FROM THE BRIDGWATER TOWN COUNCIL COLLECTION, COURTESY THE BLAKE MUSEUM)

During the period of the bridge's construction, a temporary wooden bridge on piles was used to connect the two banks, placed more or less where the present Town Bridge now stands.

At the same time, the quaysides, which were also in a poor state of repair, were brought up to standard. This work required an Act of Parliament, part of which read:

... narrow, incommodious and dangerous to passengers, carriages and cattle, passing over the same and the said bridge is very ancient in want of repair and so constructed that the navigation of the said river is rendered very inconvenient and dangerous.

The £4,000 cost of the bridge was met by raising tolls on the roads into the town. The bridge, which lasted 90 years, was replaced with the current Town Bridge.

Roads need to be maintained. Historically, no one bothered. Travel was so limited that green tracks were sufficient for foot and horse travellers, who caused little wear and tear. The introduction of wheeled traffic changed that. As early as 1501 we can find evidence of local merchants paying for the maintenance of the road between Bridgwater and Taunton. By the early-eighteenth century the Turnpike Act had been introduced, which allowed tolls to be charged for the maintenance of the roads. In 1730 the Bridgwater Turnpike Trust was set up, a body which was to last until 1870, when the Motor Car Act was introduced.

The first roads to be turnpiked were those to Taunton (which was re-aligned at the same time, leaving us with the Old Taunton Road), Langport and the Minehead Road, which ran through Wembdon village (Quantock Road did not exist at that time). These turnpike routes followed existing roads and no new ones were introduced except for Bristol Road. Previously the traveller to Bristol would take the Bath Road to Crandon Bridge and fork left over Puriton Hill to Pawlett.

Roads around Bridgwater soon improved in standard, with turnpike roads from the town to Thurloxton, East Brent, Nether Stowey, the Piper's Inn, Langport Bridge, Bishop's Lydeard and Spaxton.

A few milestones and notices indicating the Turnpike Trust can still be seen along these routes.

The Architectural Legacy

Originally known as Chandos Street, one of the finest Georgian streets outside Bath, Bridgwater's Castle Street, was built between 1720 and 1723 on the instruction of the Duke of Chandos, then one of the world's wealthiest men, arguably wealthier at the time than the king himself. It had been almost 40 years since the Civil War and the destruction of the castle. James Bridges, Duke of Chandos and the Consul-General of Queen Anne's Army, had been charged with the task of the disposal of the castle. It was under his instructions that Castle Street was built by local craftsmen under the architect Benjamin Holloway, who also, in 1720, built The Lions on the West Quay for his own use.

Whilst Castle Street looks uniform in design, closer inspection shows that each doorway is of individual character. Likewise with the porches and windows. Another legacy left by the Duke of Chandos was the glass kiln near Valetta Place. It was one of a number of failed attempts by the duke to develop various industries in Bridgwater. His soap works failed in 1725, as did his Eastover-based distillery. The glass kiln, built in 1726, was abandoned in 1733 but later resurrected as a pottery kiln until 1942, having served as a prison for French captives in the Napoleonic Wars. It was destroyed in 1942 when hardcore was required to extend the runways at Westonzoyland aerodrome when the Americans joined the war. It was a sad end to a building, the stump of which was granted listed building status in 1977.

Bell Foundries

In Dr Raven's *The Bells of England*, he refers to Bridgwater as one of the limited number of towns with a bell foundry; the eighteenth century saw bell manufacturing at a peak in the town. Among the foundries were those in the table below.

Thomas Bayley, Street & Co.	*1738–73*	*Bridgwater, Charlynch, Enmore , Hinton St George (where there is also a Bayley weather cock), Lopen, Northover Church at Tintinhull, St Bartholomew's at Crewkerne, five at All Saints in Langport and a candelabrum at Old Cleeve.* *Bridgeton, New Jersey — see story below.*
Thomas Pike	*1776–81*	*Tintinhull, Tenby*
George and Thomas Davis	*1782–99*	*Enmore (2), Hinton St George, Middlezoy, Tintinhull, Stoke sub Hambdon.*
J. Kingston joined by Isaac Kingston (1801), Thomas (1808) and Edmund (1831)	*1798–1829*	*Enmore, Shepton Beauchamp, Crewkerne, Huish Episcopi, Stockland Bristol (4) and Hinton St George*
Unknown		*Chedzoy*

Castle Street.

Bells were certainly being produced in Bridgwater much earlier than the above, but the eighteenth century was the boom time. As early as 1538 there were five bells, cast in Bridgwater, hanging in Charlynch Church. One of those same bells, made in the fourteenth century, now hangs in a church in Reykjavik in Iceland. Even earlier, in the late-thirteenth century, there are records of funds being raised for a bell to be cast in the town which weighed in at 16cwt (800kg).

It can be seen from the table that, as one firm closed, another opened. Each successive company used the same premises in St Mary Street.

The Legend of the Little Liberty Bell

I recently discovered that a bell cast by Thomas Bayley was destined for Bridgeton in the state of New Jersey in the United States, where it is now known as the Little Liberty Bell. The bell was cast in 1763 for the inhabitants of Cohansey Bridge Town, later to be known as Bridgeton, in West New Jersey. It was lashed onto a framework, loaded onto a wagon drawn by a team of horses and taken down to the West Quay, where it was loaded aboard a brig, the *Governor Franklin*, named after the governor of New Jersey.

On arriving in the States, at Cohansey Bridge Town (150 inhabitants), the leading citizen of the town, Ebenezer Miller, was there to inspect the new arrival. The bell was then transferred onto an ox cart and taken up a steep hillside to the top of a bluff where stood the brick-built Cumberland County Court House with its high-peaked belfry. The bell was hoisted into position.

In the years that followed, turmoil visited the States as the War of Independence took hold. On 7 August 1776 a courier arrived in the town with a printed Declaration of Independence, hot off the press in Philadelphia, some 50 miles away. Jonathan

The Little Liberty Bell, cast in Bridgwater but residing in Bridgeton, USA.

Elmer ordered Thomas Harris to ring the bell to summon the town's inhabitants so they could hear the news. The bell was rung again in celebration and was declared to be 'The Little Liberty Bell'.

Slavery

Whilst America was gaining its independence, it had yet to experience its own civil war which, although originally about taxation on cotton, became a major issue where slavery was concerned. In 1785 Bridgwater had its own part to play in the abolition of slavery. The town mayor and other citizens sent the first petition to Parliament for the abolition of the African slave trade. Thomas Clarkson, in his *History of the Rise, Progress and Accomplishment of the Abolition of the African Slave-Trade*, wrote:

In the year 1785 we find other coadjudicators coming before our view, but these in a line different from that in which any other belonging to this class has yet moved. Mr George White, a clergyman of the Established Church, suggested to Mr Wm Tuckett, the mayor of Bridgwater, where they resided, and to others of that town, the propriety of petitioning Parliament for the abolition of the slave trade. This petition was agreed upon, and was as follows:

'The humble petition of the inhabitants of Bridgwater shows that...' This petition was presented by the Honourable Mr Poulett, and Alexander Hood, Esq., who were Members for the town of Bridgwater. It was ordered to lie on the table. The answer which these gentlemen gave to their constituents relative to the reception of it in the House of Commons is worthy of notice. There did not appear, say they in their common letter, 'the least disposition to pay any further attention to it. Every one almost say the abolition of the slave trade must immediately throw the West India Islands into convulsions and soon complete their utter ruin. Thus they will not trust Providence for its protection for so pious an undertaking.'

The petition, although having failed, prompted thousands of others to follow and eventually brought about the much sought after abolition in 1807.

Entertainment

By the end of the eighteenth century, horse racing was one of the most popular forms of entertainment. The course was on Chilton Common, which was actually across the river from Chilton Trinity, reflecting how the River Parrett had changed its course. Roughly in the area where Wylds Road meets the Bristol Road, the racecourse was a mile-long circular track of fine grass. In the centre was a

An invitation to Bridgwater races 1794.

natural grandstand large enough for 3,000 spectators. The races date back to at least 1780 and were almost daily affairs by 1794, when the race card of 25 August advertised three heats of novice races for Somerset-owned hunters who had not yet won £20 in prize money and other races for novice hacks who had not yet won £50. The entrance fee was half a guinea.

Interest in the local races waned for a while but received a boost when Taunton Races were transferred to Bridgwater in 1813 and then again in 1854. All horses had to be registered at the Crown Inn before the start of the race and ran under Newmarket rules. By 1898 the Bridgwater Steeplechase and Hurdle Race were established under National Hunt rules and were run in September. In 1905, these races were abandoned and attempts to revive them on the Fairfield in 1926 met with some success but only until 1929, when the last race was run.

Other forms of eighteenth-century entertainment are indicated in the names of Bull Baiting Acre, which was one of the fields next to the Castle Fields, in the Wylds Road area, and in Coxpit Farm in East Bower.

✦ CHAPTER 7 ✦

The Nineteenth Century: Political Corruption and Economic Development

Political Corruption

Could anyone ever doubt the corruptibility of politicians? Whilst many of us may prefer to think this is a recent phenomenon, there is evidence that, in Bridgwater at least, the corruption goes back hundreds of years, particularly in connection with the party system of politics.

Throughout the seventeenth century, corruption existed in the appointment of individuals to key posts, including that of local vicar. This corruption continued into the eighteenth century, culminating in a scandalous exposure in 1869. In 1741 there were three candidates standing for election to Parliament: Vere Poulett, George Bubb Doddington and Sir Charles Wyndham. The voters, who were very limited in number, went to the Cornhill to declare the way they were giving their votes. There was no secret ballot. The recorder simply stood with the voting register on a lectern and recorded each voter's

Above, and right: *Scenes from the 1927 Pageant depicting trouble at the hustings.*
(FROM THE ROGER EVANS COLLECTION)

wishes. It was an open system, almost beyond corruption. When the votes were counted Wyndham had come bottom of the poll and immediately published an article accusing the recorder of corruption. The recorder, who was the town clerk, in order to protect his integrity, published the complete list, showing how each individual had cast his vote.

The problem was that Wyndham, a countryman, had sent his bully boys into the town to 'persuade' the local burgesses, the tradesmen of the town, to vote for him or risk loss of business because Wyndham would ensure that no one would supply them. Most of them had agreed, just to get the bully boys off their backs, and then, on the day of the poll, had voted according to their consciences. Wyndham's plan had backfired. He had now not only lost the election but had had his tactics exposed for all the electorate to see.

In 1754 Bubb Doddington spent £3,400 trying to buy the Bridgwater electorate and described his experience as follows:

All this trouble and vexation and expense flows from a set of low, worthless fellows… Spent these three days in an infamous and disagreeable compliance with the low habits of venal wretches

Having insulted the people of Bridgwater in this way, Doddington perhaps deserved to lose, which he did, and left the town, having written in his diary, 'Left the town of Bridgwater… forever!'

By the 1830s, nothing had improved, in fact corruption was so rife as to have been accepted as standard practice. The number of voters was still very limited, around 500, and the going rate for a vote was £10. In a closely fought election, the ante could go up to £50 to get the last few vital votes. Voters would often hold out, waiting for the market price to increase. However, this could backfire. If a candidate's victory was obvious, then the price could drop to nothing. Most voters simply took the cash in advance of the day and promised their support to the payer. In the election of 1835 Mr Broadwood was paying £40 per vote while his opponent, Mr Leader, was more generous at £50. The number of voters at the time was 400 and it is considered that between £20,000 and £30,000 was spent on bribes.

This illegal practice had to be kept under cover, although everyone knew that it went on. Votes would be bought and sold in the back rooms of inns. The votes were referred to as 'commodities', the name of the commodity indicating the going price, e.g. £100 was paid for a pig, £50 for a parrot. In 1831 a blacksmith was quoted as charging £50 to shoe a candidate's horse, whereupon the candidate's opponent asked for two shoes for his horse and, for £100, got the vote. Local voters would be seen entering the chosen inn to buy a pig and then leaving without it! The agents who took the money were equally referred to by pseudonyms, 'the man in the moon', 'the mysterious stranger', with the bribe referred to as 'a packet of tea'.

The Case of the Drunken Jury

Before 1832 major changes took place in the political set up. The Whig party went out of action and the Liberals emerged. At the same time the number of electors increased by 50 per cent. The Whigs and Tories having previously bribed the voters, they would now be hard pressed to find the money for the increased numbers, and so the two parties agreed to return one candidate each – uncontested. This meant that voters got no payment, which obviously proved very unpopular. In 1832 the parties agreed to return to the system of putting forward two candidates each, and hence an election was required. Both sides had to spend a great deal of money. The Tories realised they couldn't afford it and so withdrew and the voters went to the local office of the Bridgwater *Alfred* (a politically based newspaper) and complained.

The resulting riot ended in the arrest of 43 gentlemen. Rioting was a serious offence and carried deportation as a sentence, the guilty ending up in Botany Bay. Stealing a loaf of bread would get you deported; causing a riot would get you deported for the rest of your life. The arrested offenders, however, were gentlemen of the town who could afford a good barrister – Benjamin Lovibond – to defend them. The first six, sent to Taunton, got off on a technicality, so the rest were sent to Wells. Due to the small size of the court, the trial was held over two days and the accused, jury, judge and witnesses all had to share the same hotel. The Liberals put £500 behind the bar to ensure all present could have a really good time. The party continued through the night and the accused and jury alike ended up sharing beds in the drunken confusion. At the conclusion of the trial, not surprisingly, the hung-over jury found all the accused not guilty.

The accused, relieved at their release, donated a 22-inch silver salver to Benjamin Lovibond. This salver was rediscovered in the Channel Islands after the war, with no knowledge as to how it got there, and found its way back to Bridgwater, where it became part of the town's silver collection.

Disenfranchised

In May 1837 a by-election was fought. The Tory candidate, Henry Broadwood, won by 279 votes to 221. Such was the national interest in this by-election that the editor of the London *Times* chartered 15 relay horses, one at each end of a ten-mile stretch on the road to London. The voting continued throughout the day with more than the usual bribery and more than the usual fighting. On the stroke of 4 o'clock the poll was closed and the result inscribed on a paper, which was handed to the first horse rider, who was

Declaration of the poll in 1910.

(FROM THE ROGER EVANS COLLECTION)

bedecked in ribbon, as was his horse. The crowd opened and horse and rider galloped away in a cloud of dust, heading for the Piper's Inn, where the next horse waited.

Sure enough, the following day, the London *Times* arrived with the published results. But there was more news to come. The Liberals objected and proved that at least 153 votes had been paid for – as if they were not also involved in the same malpractice! The case was proven, the Tory de-seated, and the Liberal Richard Sheridan returned to Parliament. Unfortunately William IV died before Sheridan could take his seat, which meant a general election.

At the ensuing election, with two seats for MPs at Parliament, the two Tory candidates were returned with nearly 600 votes between them, leaving the Liberals with only seven. The Tories had pulled off a classic double-cross. Not only had they paid the voters to cast their votes for the Tory candidates, they had also paid them to falsely declare their loyalty to the Liberals and promise to vote Liberal without payment. What is especially interesting about this result is not the huge majority but the implication behind the statistics, which is that only seven voters were prepared to vote without payment!

Corruption surfaced again in 1865, when Henry Westropp, Tory, topped the poll and was proven to have paid for votes. Three years later the two Liberal candidates just pipped the two Tories, and they also

were proved to have paid for votes. In 1869 a Royal Commission was called for to establish the extent of the problem. After 47 days of enquiry, during which the previous five elections were investigated, a report was produced running to 1,174 pages and detailing 47,548 questions and answers. The Commission concluded that it was bad – very bad. They found evidence of corruption over at least the previous 40 years, and evidence that, if a voter was found to be incorruptible where bribes were concerned, the common practice was to get that voter so drunk that he could not make it to the poll. Corruption was so rife that there was no hope at all of ever running a fair election in the town. The Commission concluded that it would take at least two generations before a fair election could be held, and only then if the town was disenfranchised in the meantime. And so it was. The town was deprived of the right to return an MP. Before they were allowed to vote again the rules had changed and, from then on, only one MP was returned to Parliament.

The Advent of the Railway

As trade from the town increased, the traffic between Bridgwater and Bristol increased dramatically. The only route to Bristol at the start of the nineteenth century was via Bath Road, out to Crandon Bridge, turn left over Puriton Hill and down the other side to Pawlett. Bristol Road did not exist then but was introduced in 1823, for obvious reasons. What the town really needed, however was a rail link.

In 1841 the long-awaited railway came to town with the arrival, on 1 June, of the *Fireball* towing six carriages with 400 passengers from Bristol Temple Meads, a journey which had taken an hour and three-quarters. The passengers stopped at Bridgwater long enough for a champagne lunch and returned to Bristol. Almost two weeks later, on 14 June, the official opening took place, the band of the West Somerset Yeomanry, Bridgwater's own regiment, providing the musical entertainment.

Owned by the Bristol & Exeter Railway Co., the railway reached to Taunton the following year, when the Somerset Bridge was built across the Parrett. At this time the town extended no further than the end of Eastover at one end of the town and the Malt Shovel Inn, at the end of North Street, at the other. In the wake of the railway's arrival, St John Street, Edward Street, Devonshire Street and Wellington Road soon sprang up.

Since the railway temporarily reached Bridgwater but no further, it was a natural progression for the stagecoaches which served the villages and other towns to move their pick-up points to the railway station. The *Exquisite*, which served Exeter, was one of these. Its driver had become used to turning his stagecoach around at the end of the station platform, more or less where the footbridge is now. This was quite

The Railway Hotel, 1865.   (FROM THE BRIDGWATER TOWN COUNCIL COLLECTION, COURTESY THE BLAKE MUSEUM)

The Bristol & Exeter Carriage Works, 1865, a major employer in Colley Lane.

(FROM THE BRIDGWATER TOWN COUNCIL COLLECTION, COURTESY THE BLAKE MUSEUM)

Railway station staff in 1859. The top-hatted gent was the signalman.

(FROM THE BRIDGWATER TOWN COUNCIL COLLECTION, COURTESY THE BLAKE MUSEUM)

safe since the line extended no further. Unfortunately it had become such a habit that, when the line opened to Taunton, the coach driver decided to challenge the train driver as to which of them had the right of way. The coach overturned, a passenger suffered a broken ankle and the railway engine jumped the rails.

The development of the railway brought with it a need for the production of rolling stock and, in 1849, a railway carriage manufacturing works opened in Colley Lane, producing rolling stock for the two gauges of railway which existed at the time, even producing narrow carriages on broad-gauge bases in readiness for standardisation. The Bristol & Exeter Railway was eventually taken over by the Great Western Railway Co. in 1876. They also owned riverside wharves. Opened in 1845 and employing horse-drawn wagons which were replaced by steam transport in 1867, the wharves remained in use right up until the First World War. They were then used as sidings until the Second World War, when the track was taken up to provide metal for the war effort.

In close proximity to the station was the Railway Hotel, no longer in existence. The land used for the rail line and the station was previously owned by the Sidcot Charity, a Quaker organisation. They afterwards divided up the surrounding pasture land, selling it for housing development and greatly enhancing the funds of the charity. The rapid growth of such a densely populated area brought with it the need for another church in the town and St John's Church was built in 1846 with funds provided by the Revd J.M. Capes, who became its first vicar. Within 18 months he had converted to the Roman Catholic faith.

The Somerset & Dorset Joint Railway

In 1854 the Somerset & Dorset Joint Railway Co. opened a line between Highbridge and Glastonbury. This line was extended to Burnham-on-Sea in 1858, when it was envisioned that ferries would bring passengers across from Wales who could then travel on the Somerset & Dorset all the way down to Poole on the Dorset coast, where they could catch a ship to France. The scheme never succeeded but it provided a line from Burnham to Glastonbury and the opportunity to run a spur line down to Bridgwater from the newly created Edington Junction. Opening in 1890, the new line gave the opportunity for day-trippers from Bridgwater to visit Burnham beach. The terminus at the Bridgwater end was in the area where McDonalds and Sainsbury's have their outlets in 2006, and it was from here that many a Sunday-school outing provided the annual trip to the seaside, costing 9d. for adults and 6d. for children. As many as 200–300 children would be loaded into the carriages of the 9 o'clock train, then, after a day on the beach and tea at the Lifeboat Café, it was back on the train for the homeward journey.

Although the link to Edington opened in 1890, there had been an earlier attempt to open the line which turned out to be a financial scam. It was 1875 when the Bridgwater Railway Co. was formed. The argument in favour of a new railway was that nine out of 10 trains on the Bristol & Exeter Railway ran late! It was argued that it was quicker to get to London by horse and cart than via the Bristol to Exeter line with its London links. At one stage, an

Celebrating the centenary of the Somerset Central Railway. (FROM THE ROGER EVANS COLLECTION)

Water-tower at the Colley Lane ironworks, 1865.
(FROM THE BRIDGWATER TOWN COUNCIL COLLECTION, COURTESY THE BLAKE MUSEUM)

Act of Parliament declared that customers of either company could specify over which route goods would be taken. This led to Bristol & Exeter customers asking for their goods to be delivered over the Somerset & Dorset lines, since they had the swifter service. But back to 1875. In a nutshell, investors put large sums of money into the scheme and solicitors took almost as much out of it in legal fees. The appropriately named Mr Toogood, the brains behind the scheme, was persuaded by the Bristol & Exeter not to pursue the proposal on the basis that it would only result in a price war, with both companies losing out. Toogood agreed, subject to the Bristol & Exeter paying his expenses – which were enormous. In 1882 Toogood was at it again. Once again, huge sums of money, fat solicitors' fees but this time no bribe from the Bristol & Exeter and no second railway. Bridgwater had to wait until 1890 to get its second rail company.

The day the new station opened, it poured down and the celebrations were a washout. However, the company operated profitably and the first decade saw much activity, with cattle pens, toilets, stables and plate-layers' huts being constructed. A limestone quarry was opened at Cossington, taking advantage of the rail link, and the Bear Creek Oil Co. opened a depot at Bridgwater Station. A 400ft wharf was constructed along the river, on the Castle Fields side. By 1892 there were nine trains in each direction to London and Southampton on this alternative to the Bristol & Exeter, all leaving from Bridgwater North Station with its stationmaster and four porters. One errant staff member from those days was the

goods guard, who was in the habit of popping over to the Cross Rifles for a pint or two whilst the train was being prepared for departure. On the night in question, a cold October evening, the steam from the engine hung thick and low along the platform. The engine driver, seeing the newly employed porter at the rear end of the train, mistook him for the guard and waved to him, signalling that he was ready to pull out. The new porter, taking the wave as a kindly gesture, waved back, and the train pulled out without the guard.

The Somerset & Dorset operated profitably right up until the First World War, when all railways were nationalised. In 1921 the railway, which was by now the Bridgwater Railway Co., became part of the London South Western Railway, ending a 30-year period of independence. There then followed three decades of decline, by which time British Railways was in control, and in 1952 came the closure of the line to passengers. On 1 October 1954, the last goods train pulled out.

The New Town Bridge

The iron bridge of 1797 had served the town well but with the creation of the dock in 1840 and the arrival of the railway in 1841, on opposite sides of the river to each other, traffic across the iron bridge increased both in number of journeys and size of load. The old bridge, with its elliptical arch, proved too steep for the heavily-laden horse-drawn wagons. A new bridge was required with less of a gradient.

In 1883 a new bridge was opened with a 75ft

span, designed by R.C. Else and G.B. Laffan and constructed by George Moss, of Liverpool. Originally to be opened in the May of that year, the project slipped behind schedule, opening in time for the November carnival procession to be used as part of the opening ceremony. A plaque on the bridge commemorates the opening of the bridge by the mayor, Mr W.T. Holland, although it was actually his wife who cut the ribbon and led the procession up to the Town Hall for the celebratory feast. Her husband, who was rarely ill, was confined to his bed, at his West Quay Lions House home, with gout – allegedly. Local legend has it that Mrs Holland, having read his prepared speech, unexpectedly returned home to be at his bedside. This was clearly not expected, as she found him in bed with the maid!

Souvenirs from the old bridge were sold off to help cover the cost of the new one and one relic survives today – the town coat of arms, which is to be found on the portico of the Royal Clarence House building.

Further Churches and Chapels

The history of churches and chapels in the town clearly spreads across the centuries but it was in the nineteenth century that we find the greatest expansion and the most active comings and goings, especially of chapel communities. Hence, irrespective of the centuries to which they belong, I bring them all together with the exception of the Church of St Mary the Virgin and St John's Hospital,

which have their origins so deeply rooted in the medieval period.

Church of England

We have already seen how the expansion of the Eastover part of the town led to the creation of St John's Church. On the other side of the river, Holy Trinity Church had also been built on the Taunton Road, six years earlier, in 1840. Designed by Richard Carver and built of stone, it fell into disuse and was demolished in 1958 to permit the construction of Broadway from Taunton Road to North Street. Its graveyard survives as witness to its former existence. It was effectively replaced by a new church in Greenfield, the Holy and Undivided Trinity, designed by Caroe & Partners and opened in Hamp Street in 1961.

In 1882 St John's Church opened the All Saints' Church as a mission church on the Westonzoyland Road. This replaced a meeting room in Edward Street, but by 1966 the church had closed. Since then it has been used as a boys' club and for community activities. Not too far away, on the Sydenham Estate, the church of St Francis of Assisi opened on Saxon Green in 1965.

Roman Catholic

For the Roman Catholics, practising their religion was difficult for many years. Local archives record them as being reported for practising their religion during the years 1583–1613, and in 1767 a toll keeper, two other men, a cook shop proprietor and another

Holy Trinity Church, c.1910.

St John's Church. (FROM THE ROGER EVANS COLLECTION)

All Saints' Mission Church, 1914. (FROM THE ROGER EVANS COLLECTION)

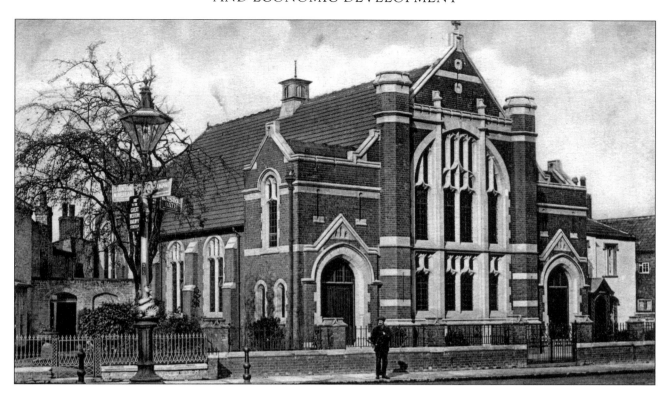

Monmouth Street Methodist Church.

lady were all reported as being Papists. In 1845 the Roman Catholic mass was being celebrated on a regular basis in a private home, but following the conversion of the Revd Capes, who had paid for and preached at St John's Church, a chapel dedicated to St Joseph was opened in Gordon Terrace in 1846, Capes once again meeting part of the cost. By 1878 the church had at least 60 members and by 1882 had moved to new premises at Binford Place, the building being extended in 1982 to accommodate its growing congregation. Meanwhile, the abandoned chapel in Gordon Terrace found a new lease of life as a workshop for the Cummins family and it was here that many of the farm carts they produced were manufactured. Linked to the Roman Catholic church, the Sisters of the Holy Rosary opened a convent in Eastcroft on Durleigh Road. It remained as a convent until 1990, when it was given a new role as a retirement home.

Baptists
The original Baptists appear to have begun their meetings in 1653. In 1692 they erected a meeting house in St Mary Street and by 1712 had 200 members. However, perhaps as the result of the minister having 'purged the church of Arminians', by 1780 their flock had diminished to fewer than 30. In 1835 a new chapel was built on the site of the old one. John Wesley, the grandfather of John and Charles Wesley, who founded the Methodist Church, had been a regular preacher at the Baptist Chapel. In 1880 the church opened a house on the West Quay for

sailors and, nearby, a temperance house. By 1907 there was an active membership in excess of 1,000. In 1965 they opened a chapel in Moorland Road on the Sydenham Estate but this closed in 1972 and became the new premises for the Salvation Army.

Methodists
John Wesley, founder with his brother of the Methodist movement, first visited the town in 1746, when he preached late on a September afternoon, and appeared regularly thereafter until 1769, albeit with a ten year gap from 1749 to 1759. When he reappeared in Bridgwater in 1760, on a miserable wet day, he described the town as 'a dead and uncomfortable place at best'. Surprisingly, after a comment like that, there were still sufficient followers to open two Wesleyan Chapels.

In 1753 a house was approved for worship. By 1800 there was a Methodist church in Eastover, a further chapel being built in King Street in 1816. The Monmouth Street Methodist Church we see today was built in 1911. Primitive Methodist chapels were also set up in Angel Crescent in 1852 and West Street in 1861, the latter being used by the Salvation Army in 1880, by which time the Methodists had moved to St John Street, probably where the Mariners' Chapel was later founded. In 1866 the Bible Christians came to the town and were based in an iron chapel on the Bath Road until they moved in 1876 to new premises in Polden Street. They practised here until 1906 and then joined the United Methodists. Their old building survives as an industrial unit.

Members of the Salvation Army outside the Citadel, where a poster proclaims the forthcoming visit of General Booth.
(FROM THE ROGER EVANS COLLECTION)

Salvation Army

The Salvation Army arrived in 1880 and were met with tremendous resistance when they used the former Methodist premises in West Street. In 1881 they moved to the Zion Chapel in Friarn Street, which had previously been used by the Independents. It was a long stay there until their move to Moorland Road in 1991, taking over the former Baptist church premises. In 1884 William Booth, the founder of the movement, visited the town.

Congregationalists

In 1864 a Congregational chapel was built in Fore Street with a capacity for 900 people, lecture rooms being added later, in 1877. The building was demolished in 1964 and, two years later, the congregation moved to new premises in West Street, now the Westfield United Reform Church.

Mariners' Chapel

Founded in 1817 for seamen, the Mariners' Chapel was eventually built in St John Street in 1837. In 1885 an attempted takeover by the Congregationalists failed when the Methodists provided preachers for the services. The influence at the chapel gradually moved towards Congregational and Baptist and it survived until 1960, when the premises were sold and converted to a motorcycle shop. The Mariners, meanwhile, was moved to premises in Moorland Road, later taken over by the Salvation Army.

Fore Street Congregational Chapel.
(FROM THE HISTORY OF BRIDGWATER BY S.G. JARMAN, 1889)

Unitarian

From all the confusion of religious upheaval in the seventeenth century, there sprung a number of new religious establishments. One of these was the Unitarian Chapel in Dampiet Street, founded in 1688, a significant year in that it was the first year when there was any reasonable freedom of practice in terms of religion. The chapel was initially established on Presbyterian lines with the Revd John Moore officiating, later to be succeeded by his son. They were followed by Matthew Towgood (1747–55) and the long-serving Thomas Watson (1755–93). Next came Mr Howel, whose sentiments were strictly Unitarian, and it is that discipline which has been

The Castle Inn, where the Order of Druids met, at the entrance to Fore Street. Slightly further along is the old gaol and opposite is Akerman's Music and Piano Warehouse.

(FROM THE BRIDGWATER TOWN COUNCIL COLLECTION, COURTESY THE BLAKE MUSEUM)

practised there ever since.

Whilst the chapel was built in 1688, a new chapel, the one which we see today, was built on the same site in 1788 and a stone taken from the original, bearing the original date, is featured. There was, in fact, an even earlier church on the site, one that was circular and seated 400 people. During the troubles, in 1683, Colonel Stawell of Cothelstone Manor raided the church, searching for weapons, and then gave instructions for it to be razed to the ground. In 1797 and 1798 Samuel Taylor Coleridge preached here, having walked from his Nether Stowey home. Another character associated with the church is Captain George Lewis Browne, who is commemorated within on a plaque. Captain Browne served with Nelson and was the assistant signals officer on HMS *Victory* at the Battle of Trafalgar. His story is fully detailed in the publications *The Forgotten Heroes of Bridgwater* and *Somerset's Forgotten Heroes*.

Quakers

John Anderton, a Bridgwater goldsmith, provides us with the first record of a local Quaker in 1658, when he held meetings at his house, a practice which continued until 1670. By 1689 a meeting house had been licensed and in 1694 the famous William Penn held a Quaker meeting at the Town Hall. A generation later, in 1722, a meeting house was built in Friarn Street which was enlarged in 1801 and is still in use.

Friendly Societies

Around the back of the Duke, or the Duke of Monmouth as most of us remember it, there is an engraving over what used to be a private entrance to a 'secret' society based at the inn. At the time the inn was called the Lamb and served as the provincial headquarters for the 'grand lodge' of Somerset Freemasons. Freemasonry began in Bridgwater at least as early as 1764, when the Perpetual Friendship Lodge was established. In 1781 another lodge was established, the Liberty and Sincerity. These Masonic lodges raised money for what they saw as worthy causes, in 1789 for a campaign to abolish slavery and in 1788 to aid the government in preparation for a war against France. In 1820 and 1822 their generosity was focused on the poor in those years of depression.

In 1791 the Perpetual Friendship Lodge moved to its Lamb Inn premises when their previous headquarters at the Swan were demolished. There they met for 74 years before moving to the Royal Clarence Hotel. Their present-day premises can be found in King Square.

Apart from Masonic Lodges, the town could boast a number of Friendly Societies: The Oddfellows met at the Albion Inn and later at the Rose and Crown in St Mary Street and the Fountain Inn on the West Quay. The Order of Foresters met at the King's Arms, the Commercial Hotel in Eastover (now the Cobblestones), the Lamb Inn, and the Albion Inn in

Westover School, c.1960.

(FROM THE ROGER EVANS COLLECTION)

St Mary Street. An Order of Druids was established at the Beaufort Arms in St John Street, and others at the Nags Head in West Street, the Masons Arms, the Punch Bowl Inn on the corner of West Quay and Fore Street, Mansion House Inn in the High Street, the King's Arms on the West Quay and the Castle Inn in Binford Place. A whole host of other Friendly Societies came and went, mostly based at inns except, of course, in the case of the temperance societies.

Education

Mention has already been made of the earliest educational centres associated with the St John's Hospital and the Free Grammar School endowed by Queen Elizabeth. By 1819 the school had no pupils. However, another school had been established in Mount Street following a bequest in the 1723 of Dr John Morgan. In 1816 the school increased to 300 pupils when additional classes were made available. The school moved to Durleigh Road in 1930 and remained the town's grammar school until 1973.

Among the town's private schools were Snook's Writing School (1793) and Mr Gill's Writing School plus, numerous other smaller schools and Sunday schools and, by 1822, five boarding schools. By the middle of the nineteenth century there was a National School for boys in Mount Street and another for girls in Northgate and the two merged in 1891. From 1937 this was known as St Mary's School and survives today, having moved to its Park Road location in 1973.

For the less well off, in 1846, there was a school in the Union Workhouse, where around 60 children were taught. The following year St John's Church School was built and received 240 children. In 1975 it transferred to new premises on the Westonzoyland Road and became the St John and St Francis School.

The first Roman Catholic School was that of St Joseph's, which was founded in 1856 in two cottages in Gordon Terrace, convenient for the church. In 1882 it occupied the premises of the former mission church but the following year moved to Binford Place and there remained until 1918, by which time it was used for Sunday school only. It reopened in 1940, catering for the influx of wartime refugees but was still not recognised by the county authority. In 1963 it moved to new premises at Park Road and remains there to this day, with around 250 pupils.

In 1870 a school board was established and in its wake came additional schools. The first of these was Eastover School in Cornboro Place, built in 1870 and opened in 1873. Within two years it had over 600 pupils and, by 1899, over 1,300. By 1947 numbers had dropped to 475. The school survives today with around 350 pupils. It was at this school that I received my own primary education, progressing, aged ten, to the grammar school.

The second board school was in Albert Street, founded in 1880. In 1958 it became Friarn School and in 1978 the juniors migrated to the former Westover School premises, the infants joining them a few years later. The school survives today under the name of Westover Green. Westover School served as the town's secondary modern school until its closure in 1973. By that time other secondary schools had opened: Hamp in 1956, its name changing to Blake the following year; Sydenham in 1961, later changing its name to East Bridgwater; and Chilton Trinity in 1966. These all joined the comprehensive system in 1973, when Dr Morgan's Grammar School for Boys and the girls' grammar school ceased to exist, the former becoming Haygrove Comprehensive.

From 1860 tertiary education was initially served by the Bridgwater School of Arts in George Street. Another art school was founded in 1888 in Queen Street and then moved to Blake Street, where the Bridgwater Arts and Technical College was established. In 1959 new premises, built on the Broadway to house the technical college, were soon outgrown. In 1978 new premises were built at Bath Road and the college has been based there ever since, continually

Bridgwater Free Library, endowed by Andrew Carnegie, c.1907.   (FROM THE ROGER EVANS COLLECTION)

expanding and now at a size where the original establishments are completely dwarfed. In 2004 it also took responsibility for Cannington College, formerly the Somerset Farm Institute.

Newspapers and Libraries

The nineteenth century was a boom period for newspapers and libraries. The first library opened in Taunton Road in 1856, another in St John Street in 1860 and yet another in West Street in 1861. There was also a 'Literary and Scientific Institution' in George Street, with over 1,500 volumes, and a museum, plus a 'Free Library and Reading Rooms' within the Town Hall, with over 2,500 volumes.

The public library as we know it today had to wait until 1905 and was the result of an endowment from the Scottish-American steel magnate Andrew Carnegie. With its dome, it was designed to reflect the image of the Cornhill and was an octagonal Edwardian variation on the market building.

The town could boast many newspapers but most of them had a political purpose. The first paper to bear the name of the town in its title was the *Taunton and Bridgwater Journal* which, published by James Savage and financed by the local Conservatives, first appeared in March 1811 and lasted until 1816. The *Journal* was succeeded by the *Alfred*, which was published on Mondays and ran from August 1831 to December 1933. Its full title was *The Alfred, London Weekly Journal and Bridgwater and Somerset General Advertiser*! Printed in St Mary Street, it was owned by John Bowen, who had a specific interest in the

atrocious conditions of the local workhouse. It was edited by Harry Clement Heard until it was incorporated into the *Dorset County Chronicle and Somerset General Advertiser*, published in Dorset, hence losing its local identity.

The first paper purely for Bridgwater was the *Bridgwater and Somersetshire Herald*, published each Wednesday by George Aubrey in Fore Street. It survived from 1825 to August 1831. This left a gap until January 1846, when the *Bridgwater Times* was published. Printed in Fore Street and lasting until September 1861, the paper was owned by Samuel Bowditch West and edited by George Thomas Donisthorpe. Its first edition carried a report describing how its reporter had been denied access to a town council meeting.

The oldest surviving newspaper is the *Bridgwater Mercury*. It was originally run by W.A. Woodley, a clergyman's son, who was petitioned by prominent townspeople to get it started. This was on 25 June 1857, in Ball's Lane, now George Street, before moving to King Street. During 1859 and 1860 it underwent a number of name changes but always had Mercury somewhere in the title. Mr Dunsford joined the paper as its editor in 1865. It was whilst he was still in that role that, in 1883, tragedy struck both the newspaper and his family. On 25 June a fire broke out on the paper's premises, sadly destroying all of the paper's historic records. Upstairs, in their living accommodation, Dunsford's three daughters died in the flames and his wife died as the result of injuries sustained when she leapt from the upstairs window, attempting to land on a neighbour's bed.

Meanwhile, in 1871, a newspaper was launched entitled the *Bridgwater Gazette, Somerset and Devon Chronicle and West of England Advertiser*. Printed in Tiverton under the control of George Rookes and produced by James Bulgin for the Liberal cause, this became the *Bridgwater Independent* in July 1885. It was then published in George Street on Fridays and survived until June 1933, when it was bought out by the *Mercury*.

A *Bridgwater Standard* was also published by Conrad Stokes in St John Street, lasting from October 1861 to March 1870. In 1885 the short-lived *Bridgwater Guardian* was published in the old *Gazette* office in Fore Street as a voice for the Conservatives. Although belonging to the twentieth century, for completeness I mention here the *Bridgwater Echo* (1902 to 1904) and the *Slave Market News*, which ran from October 1924 to July 1936 and was published in Bridgwater.

Utilities

By an Act of Parliament of 1834 Bridgwater was permitted to introduce gas lighting to the streets, replacing the previous oil-lamps, lit by one John Gillingham and his son. The introduction of gas for street lighting brought the added benefit of gas then being available for domestic and commercial premises. Each evening the lamplighter would walk the streets and turn the gas-lights on and then, on his bicycle with his long lamplighter's pole, would switch them off as daylight broke. The first gas-lamp in the town was lit by Mr W.J. Ford at the premises of Edward Jefferies, a chemist in Fore Street. The first public building to use gas lighting was the town theatre, situated in Back Street (Clare Street), a replica of the Adelphi in London. A theatre programme of 1837 announced that the theatre would be 'brilliantly lighted with gas'. The theatre was eventually pulled down and replaced with a row of cottages called Theatre Place.

The local gasworks were erected in what is now Old Taunton Road where tar, with its distinctive smell, was produced as a by-product. This was used on road surfaces as early as 1908 but was not seriously trialled until 1921, when it was used on the stretch of road between Bridgwater and North Petherton. The trial was successful and in 1925 Trinidad Lake Asphalt was laid around the town centre roads, bringing with it the end of the bonfire on the Cornhill, since asphalt burns very readily.

Water also became an issue as the town began to grow and in December 1879 the Bridgwater Corporation Waterworks was opened at Ashford Reservoir near Cannington. Durleigh (1938) and Hawkridge Reservoirs (1962) were to follow many years later. Until the creation of the Ashford Reservoir, the town had been almost entirely dependent on locally bored wells for its water-

Manley the lamplighter with his oil-lamp, 1865.
(FROM THE BRIDGWATER TOWN COUNCIL COLLECTION, COURTESY THE BLAKE MUSEUM)

supply. From Ashford, water was pumped up to an underground holding tank at Sandford beyond the top of Wembdon Hill, still visible today. This ensured a good enough head of water to provide the required pressure.

In earlier times, back in 1694, Richard Lowbridge of Stourbridge had been granted permission to take water from the Durleigh Brook by means of an engine and to convey it to a cistern which was built over the High Cross at the Cornhill. The part of the brook from which the water was extracted was known as Friars and was owned by George Balch, who took ownership of the supply system which, in 1709, used elm pipes to convey the water.

Law and Order

Bridgwater's Regiment

Bridgwater was well served with the instruments of law and order. Not only did it have its own police force, it also had its own regiment. During the years when Napoleon posed a threat, each district had its own militia. In 1803 20,000 men enrolled in the Yeomanry or Volunteer Corps in Somerset alone, from a population of just under 90,000.

The West Somerset Yeomanry marching out across Town Bridge on their way to the Boer War, 1899.
(FROM THE BRIDGWATER TOWN COUNCIL COLLECTION, COURTESY THE BLAKE MUSEUM)

The Wiltshire and Dorset Bank at 14 The Cornhill, 1865. The manager, Captain John Ford, was the commanding officer of the Bridgwater Yeomanry.
(FROM THE BRIDGWATER TOWN COUNCIL COLLECTION, COURTESY THE BLAKE MUSEUM)

The Police Station was in the High Street in 1880.
(FROM THE BRIDGWATER TOWN COUNCIL COLLECTION, COURTESY THE BLAKE MUSEUM)

In 1794 Bridgwater already had two companies of volunteer infantry. The Bridgwater Volunteers started with 60 privates in each company and by 1795 had their own quartermaster and surgeon. Their adjutant was John Crosse, who was paid 8s. a day including 2s. for his horse. Their commandant was the MP, Lt-Col Jeffreys Allen. That same year, Lady Poulett presented the Volunteers with their colours. The regiment grew to five companies of 70 men each and their duties included escorting French prisoners from Plymouth to Bristol. In 1807 they agreed to transfer to the local militia.

In 1865, there is the first mention of the Bridgwater Troop of the West Somerset Yeomanry, commanded by Lt-Col C.K.K. Tynte. In 1868 Bridgwater's Lt Carslake of the Yeomanry Cavalry won a national rifle-shooting contest and was given a hero's welcome on his return. Escorted by the Yeomanry Cavalry, he was carried on a carriage with bands playing and the Stowey troops bearing drawn swords.

The Borough Constabulary, 1834–1940
It is hard to imagine that the town once had its own police force, independent of other forces. The old police station and gaol, established in 1834, were in Fore Street. The gaol had separate accommodation for men and women, overseen by James Bussell. The town police force consisted of the chief constable, two sergeants and ten constables, governed by the Watch Committee. In 1875 they moved to the High Street where they remained until 1911, when they settled in Northgate in what is now the magistrates' court house adjacent to the current police station building. It was a convenient site, being midway between the workhouse and the brewery.

In October 1940 the force was finally merged into the county constabulary and the present building was erected in 1966, after an embarrassing disaster where the partly erected construction collapsed.

Hard Times

The Bridgwater Workhouses
From 1770 to 1833 there had been a continuous programme of land improvement: draining the moors, raising river banks, improving navigation and enclosing agricultural land. It was land enclosure that led to thousands of agricultural workers being unemployed and desperately struggling to survive. The number of destitute people was such that Bridgwater could boast two workhouses, the last place on earth where anyone would want to go – and for many it was just that – their last place on earth.

The first workhouse was in Old Taunton Road, near the junction with St Saviours Avenue. This was the parish workhouse and dates back to 1693, when the south gate almshouse was rebuilt, part of which was afterwards used as a workhouse. By 1820 the whole building was a parish poorhouse and in 1831 typically held 86 people. Conditions were harsh, crowded and unhygienic. Within a period of only

The original Bridgwater Workhouse in Taunton Road in 1865. The wall graffiti 'Westropp forever' is a reference to the MP at the centre of the 1869 election scandal.

(FROM THE BRIDGWATER TOWN COUNCIL COLLECTION, COURTESY THE BLAKE MUSEUM)

eight months, 39 of the 155 inmates died from small pox and dysentery.

Then came 1834 and the Poor Law Amendment Act, within two years of which 17 Poor Law Unions had been set up, run by governors under the control of a commission. In other words they were run by remote politicians rather than local people. These governors focused on keeping down the costs.

This was the problem faced by Bridgwater's second workhouse. This was established in 1837 at Northgate, where the Enterprise Centre now stands, as the Union Workhouse, covering 40 parishes from Shapwick to Nether Stowey. It was a white brick, stuccoed building holding 388 inmates. Once again conditions were harsh but at least there was some heating and lighting and three insubstantial meals a

The Union Workhouse at Northgate in 1890.

(FROM THE BRIDGWATER TOWN COUNCIL COLLECTION, COURTESY THE BLAKE MUSEUM)

day. Their diet would typically include 8oz of bread (six for the women) and a pint and a half of gruel.

It was a bleak existence. Conditions were crowded, dirty and frightening. Children slept six to a bed and 50 to a room measuring 27ft by 15ft. The elderly and infirm were sent to the poorhouse where, though conditions were not much better, the inmates did not have to work. In the workhouse, they did, mostly crushing stones used to improve the roads.

In 1893 such was the demand on the workhouse that 61 tramps were admitted in one week. In both workhouses the principle was followed that no inmate should ever experience better conditions than the worst of those experienced by anyone in work. In other words, there had to be a real incentive not to be there. Despite that, the establishment was full of the dregs of society mingled with those who had simply fallen on misfortune. For the latter, the admission of entire families came as a severe shock, with the immediate separation of men into one dormitory, women into another and children into a third. Even adults had to sleep two to a bed. Cramped conditions and appalling diets caused sickness and diarrhoea. Weakened inmates easily fell prey to diseases which were endemic. The dead were rapidly removed from their beds to make room for the next inmate. The high death rates of 1837 and 1838 could have been avoided simply with a change of diet – but the law wouldn't allow it.

Reducing the food available to inmates had reduced the running costs by £5,000 a year. The increased rate of deaths was convenient in that each death solved a problem. This was the attitude taken by those who understood what was going on. There was a feeling of 'the less said, the better'. The workhouse log-book recorded that everything was satisfactory 'under the circumstances'.

John Bowen did not agree. A local man, he had travelled the world and worked as an engineer, a journalist and a wine merchant. Ill health had

The Lamb Inn, 1865, where future emigrants booked their passage to a new world.

(FROM THE BRIDGWATER TOWN COUNCIL COLLECTION, COURTESY THE BLAKE MUSEUM)

brought him back to his home town of Bridgwater and he developed an interest in local affairs. His outspoken views about the conditions in the workhouses brought him much criticism. Nonetheless, he joined the Board of Governors of the Bridgwater Parish Union and saw the conditions for himself. He was appalled. He found terrified, disease-ridden occupants, their bodies emaciated. He resigned his position and set about publishing his findings. Letters to *The Times* and Parliament, detailing 27 deaths in six months, and how 94 deaths from dysentery had been caused by the change of diet to a cheaper one, just brought him more criticism. 'Is killing in a Union Workhouse criminal if sanctioned by the Poor Law Commission?' was the title of one article. At the same time, the Board of Governors congratulated the workhouse chairman for saving £4,843!

Thanks to Bowen raising public awareness, an enquiry was held – but the panel consisted of members of the Poor Law Commission, who declared themselves innocent and Bowen to be an agitator. Bowen took his arguments to the House of Lords, presenting statistics which soon became public knowledge, showing that half the inmates had died in one winter compared with a death rate of only 3 per cent for prison inmates. Little changed – but at least the situation got no worse. The workhouse records for 1843 show local women working in the fields at a wage of 4s. a week plus 3 pints of cider a day.

In 1948 the Union Workhouse was transferred to the National Health Service and became a hospital known in 1990 as Blake Hospital, the name of Northgate being dropped and with it the stigma associated with the workhouse.

Emigration

For many impoverished members of the community, emigration was perhaps an opportunity to escape the hardships at home. For those who could pay the fare, emigration to Australia, New Zealand, Canada or America was a possibility. Assisted passage was offered to the fit and able, to help pioneer the colonies. All the emigrant had to find was the money for a decent trunk in which to store clothes and the fare to Plymouth or London, from which the emigrant ships departed. Agricultural workers were followed by tradesmen and skilled workers.

When the railway arrived, in 1841, the situation altered. Instead of needing the fare to Plymouth, London or Liverpool, the potential emigrant only needed to get to the railway station – and most of them could walk that. So the workhouse governors grasped this opportunity, pointing as many of their inmates as possible to the emigration ships. Even before that, it was often cheaper to pay the fare to a port rather than to feed the inmates. For those sailing from Liverpool, the firm of W. Tapscott & Co. made

George Williams Memorial Hall, 1907.   (FROM THE ROGER EVANS COLLECTION)

the necessary arrangements through their agent, W. Tiver, who was based at the Lamb Inn. Even the shipbuilding industry became involved, with ships built in Bridgwater specifically to take emigrants to New York. At least three ships departed from Bridgwater for that destination in 1852. So successful was the emigration programme that the scales tipped the other way and a labour shortage arose resulting, in 1853, in rising wages.

Cholera

Unfortunately, soon after the railway arrived, so did cholera. In 1849 there was a serious epidemic and almost every street in the town was hit, with more than 200 lives lost to the disease; 30 in West Street, 29 in Union Street, 19 in Mogg's Buildings and Monmouth Street, 17 in Albert Street, 13 in Bath

Road, 13 in Prickett's Lane, 9 in Honeysuckle Alley (off Market Street), 9 in Bristol Road and lesser numbers elsewhere. It is quite noticeable that the greatest impact was in those areas which were most densely populated. Strict controls were imposed on people moving around the town, with residents barred from leaving their homes if infection already existed within. In St John's churchyard is a corner grave with the inscription:

In memory of the decease of 88 persons from cholera, 1849. From plague, pestilence and sudden death; good Lord, deliver us.

Against a background of poverty and need, the Salvation Army played its part and was already established in the town by 1880; General Booth paid

A brickyard steam engine, c.1910.
(FROM THE ROGER EVANS COLLECTION)

A mini-train at a Bridgwater brickyard, c.1960.
(FROM THE ROGER EVANS COLLECTION)

Outside the cattle market at Penel Orlieu lay the smashed cart and tiles from the 1896 strike riot.
(FROM THE BRIDGWATER TOWN COUNCIL COLLECTION, COURTESY THE BLAKE MUSEUM)

The Fanny Jane *moored at Barham's Yard to be loaded with tiles.* (FROM THE ROGER EVANS COLLECTION)

a visit in 1884. Another well-known name connecting a religious group with Bridgwater is that of George Williams. Born in Dulverton in 1821, the son of a farmer, at the age of 15 he moved to Bridgwater as an apprentice to Henry William Holmes, a draper with a staff of 30. By 1837 Williams had joined the Zion Chapel in Friarn Street and become a devout Christian. In 1841 he left for London and there was to found the Young Men's Christian Association, opening the first branch in 1944; the Bridgwater branch opening in 1859.

The organisation soon grew to be one of the largest in the world. In 1887 the George Williams Memorial Hall was built for the YMCA on the corner of Eastover and Salmon Parade, on the site of the Globe Hotel, which had been destroyed by fire a few years earlier. George Williams was knighted in 1894 and died in 1905. Sadly, the magnificent building erected in his honour was allowed to fall into a state of disrepair and, to the shame of the local authority, was demolished, Bridgwater losing one of its best-loved landmarks.

Industry

The Brick and Tile Trade

For much of the nineteenth and twentieth centuries, the brick and tile industry provided the financial backbone to the town. From medieval times local clay had been used for making bricks, but it was not until the end of the seventeenth century that the

potential for clay as a commercial product was realised. There is a record of a Bridgwater brick-maker emigrating to the West Indies in 1655 and in 1687 a corporation property was being rebuilt with bricks from Mr Balch's yard. Such early developers as the Duke of Chandos had spotted the potential for clay bricks to be used as building materials, and this can be witnessed in the fine architecture of Castle Street. In those days, the clay was simply dug from wherever the building was being constructed and kiln-fired on the spot.

The present-day police station marks the spot where the first commercial brickyard was formed, the next being at Hamp (1709) and a third at Crowpill

A Bridgwater brickyard, c.1950.

(FROM THE ROGER EVANS COLLECTION)

A brickyard steam lorry, c.1920.

(FROM THE ROGER EVANS COLLECTION)

(1720). The hand-made bricks from these sites can be seen in Friarn Street, Dampiet Street and St Mary Street. More yards sprang up along the river as demand increased and, by the end of the eighteenth century, brick making was recognisable as an industry. By 1776 the Sealey family had a yard at Hamp. There were now permanent buildings with purpose-built up-draught kilns producing bricks which would be used as far away as ten miles, rather than adjacent to their place of production. This industrialisation led to improved standards, better-quality bricks and a more reliable supply. There was demand from further afield and brickyards sprang up from Burnham-on-Sea to Burrowbridge, thanks to the silt laid down there over thousands of years.

Clay varied from area to area, the clay at Chilton Trinity being particularly good for tile manufacture. Despite the limited geographic spread, the centre of the industry remained focused on Bridgwater, those listed below being among the recognised manufacturers:

The main products were the familiar red bricks and the popular Double Roman roof tiles, for which William Symons can take the credit. The kilns for firing these items could take up to 5,000 at a time and the temperature had to be just right if the tiles were not to crack in the firing process. The kilns would be loaded with faggots of wood and around 10 tons of coal. After four days, the kilns would be sealed to extinguish the fire and left for four days to cool.

In addition to bricks and tiles, ornamental gable ends were also produced and fine examples of these can still be seen, in particular in St John Street. These products ended up all over the world: the Bronx in New York, China, Canada, Australia and New Zealand. So great was the trade that in 1903 a new wharf was built to take the cargoes. My father was serving in North Africa during the Second World War and, on entering Alexandria after heavy shelling, was surprised to discover Symons roof tiles amongst the bomb damage. North Africa is a long way to take heavy cargoes like bricks and tiles but they were often an economic alternative to wasteful ballast.

Another example of a far-flung brick came when I received an email from a Brazilian University which was carrying out a maritime archaeological exploration of a ship sunk off the coast of Brazil. One of the artefacts recovered was a brick inscribed 'J.B. Hammill. Manufactured in Bridgwater'. The dimension of the brick indicated that it was a firebrick, another Bridgwater product, used in ships' galleys to prevent the outbreak of fire. Hammill's was sited right next door to a shipbuilding yard. The years in which these bricks were produced under the Hammill name proved that the ship could not have been sunk prior to those dates. Later evidence narrowed the timeframe in which the ship could have disappeared and it was eventually identified as a ship from Bristol – thanks to the Bridgwater brick.

Life was hard in the brickyards. At one time, half the male population of the town were employed in the industry. During the winter the ground would be too hard to dig and half of the workforce would be laid off. My own maternal grandfather was a Welsh miner who worked in the mines in the winter and the Bridgwater clay pits in the summer. It was in Bridgwater that he met my grandmother. The pay was poor and the days were long and hard. Families struggled and it was normal for children to work to supplement the family income. A by-law was eventually introduced prohibiting children under the age

Bridgwater Brickyard Locations

John Sealey	Hamp
Colthurst and Symons	Castle Fields, Burnham, Somerset Bridge, Somerset Yard, Screech Owl, Puriton and Combwich
John Browne	Chilton Tile Factory, Old Taunton Road, Dunwear Chilton Old Yard and Pawlett
John Browne and William Champion	Hamp
John Symons	Saltlands
William Maidment	Parrett Works (Bristol Road)
John Board	Wylds Road
Barham Brothers	East Quay
H.J. and C. Major	Salmon Parade, Taunton Road and Colley Lane
W. Robins	Parrett Way
J.B. Hammill (previously R. Ford)	Chilton Trinity

of 13 from working in the clay pits; the age was raised to 15 in 1947.

The work being so seasonal, winter unemployment levels were incredibly high, hence the need to establish the workhouse at Northgate. By 1840 there were 1,300 brickyard workers in Bridgwater and by 1850 the number of sites within two miles of the town centre had grown to 16. Conditions were so poor that by the end of the nineteenth century the time was right for trade unionism. From 1870 to 1890, union membership jumped from 4 per cent to 25 per cent of the work force. Brickyard bosses argued that low wages were essential for the survival of the yards while the workers argued that better wages were essential for the survival of their families; it was that serious, there being no social welfare, only the workhouse.

In 1886 an unsuccessful strike ended after eight weeks, the employers having refused to negotiate and hunger driving the workforce back having achieved nothing except eight weeks with no wages. In 1890 there was a repeat of the industrial action but to much greater effect when 600 workers withdrew their labour. Once again the workforce were driven back by hunger, but now they had grown in confidence as a union movement. A further strike in 1893 was followed by two years during which the brickyard workers moved towards joining the Dock, Wharf, Riverside & General Workers Union.

The Brickyard Strike of 1896

In 1896 the industrial action came to a head when the entire workforce walked out in a prolonged strike which began on 19 May, when the union leader handed in a claim for an extra 6d. per day to Henry James Major. He refused to negotiate, adopting a position of intransigence. On 26 May the notice to strike was issued and 800 workers, other than those on the picket lines, were rendered idle.

On 8 June, at a rally in Cranleigh Gardens, a promise of 9s. a week strike pay was coupled with the demand that all strike action be kept within the law. There were a number of marches through the streets in the ensuing days and the mayor unsuccessfully tried to bring the two sides together, Mr Major still refusing to negotiate. On 23 June a mass picket gathered at Barham's Yard on the East Quay and Inspector Barnett led his officers into the fray. Three workers were arrested and charged with intimidation, receiving deliberately punitive fines. This undoubtedly stirred up even more bad feeling and additional police forces were drafted in. At the end of June, Ben Tillett, a renowned trade union leader, was called in to add weight to the cause. A mass rally was called at Cranleigh Gardens, where a huge crowd gathered and tempers were close to breaking point.

The following day, a procession of carts carrying tiles, on its way from Dunwear, was challenged by the strikers. When they were informed that the tiles were destined for the hospital they only too willingly granted free passage. When, however, it was realised that the carts were going beyond the hospital and on to Wembdon, the strikers seized the cart. The police were called in to retrieve the load and ensure its safe passage but the strikers recaptured the cart, 26 of them being arrested and appearing in court.

The next day, police numbers had swelled with the addition of 100 or more officers. Harris and Tapscott were demanding that the council send the police in to take the cart. Hostility and tempers were running high. At 7p.m. troops from the Gloucestershire Regiment arrived at the railway station and marched, with reversed bayonets, to the Town Hall, where they were billeted with the hundreds of extra police reinforcements. Requests for them to be billeted in the hotels and inns had met with the doors of those establishment being barred and locked, local sympathy being clearly with the strikers. At 9p.m. all hell broke loose as the police charged the strikers with night sticks in an attempt to take the cart. The strikers responded by hurling tiles as missiles. The police were forced back and besieged in the Town Hall along with the troops and councillors.

At 3a.m. the mayor, Henry W. Pollard (founder of the local building firm), went to the Town Hall entrance and read the Riot Act as the soldiers, with bayonets fixed, forced their way through the strikers, clubbing them with their rifle butts. A surge of police followed, this tactic of force and surprise dispersing the crowd. Injuries were high and included that suffered by a young female reporter, who failed to move quickly enough when the rush came. With this action Bridgwater came under military rule for the first time since Cromwell. Two days later a union ballot was held and the vote, to the amazement of the brickyard bosses, went in favour of continuing the strike.

The financial burden of the strike had been enormous, both in terms of policing costs and for the strikers. Strike pay had diminished to 5s. a week and had nearly run out. On 5 July the strikers buckled under the financial hardship and voted for a return to work. The following year wages were increased from 12s. to 15s. per week and the working day reduced to just 12 hours.

The brickyard industry underpinned the local economy for decades, until the end of the Second World War. Although it was already in decline with home market competition, the regeneration of war-torn Europe heralded the automation of brick-making, a process for which the local clay was too heavy, being too stiff in its consistency to pass through the brick-making machines. Alternative products, such as concrete blocks, also ate into the market. Competition from the London Brick Co. finally saw off the brickyards in 1965, when Barham Brothers 'fired' for the last time and, in 1970,

Colthurst Symons closed their Castle Fields works.

Within the boundaries of the borough, 55 acres of deep pits remained as the brickyard legacy, an industry which, at its peak, produced 17,000,000 bricks per year. Over the decades, these pits have mostly been used as landfill on which supermarkets and the local college have been built. Some remain beyond the town boundaries, such as those at Chilton Trinity, Dunwear and Bath Road, and now provide such recreational facilities as fishing waters.

Bath Brick

Despite its name, Bath Brick was a Bridgwater product. Anywhere the British Army went, the Bath Brick went likewise. It started in 1820, when it was discovered that, by using silt from the river bank, bricks could be made which, when scraped, would produce a gritty substance suitable for scouring metal. A predecessor to Vim and Ajax, it was the introduction of those brands which killed the market for the Bath Brick.

The river carries a heavy burden of silt which contains an algae as well as alluvial grit. This is deposited on each tide as a layer of slimy yellow matter. Within a mile either side of the Town Bridge, where the particle size of the grit and the algae content are perfect for making Bath Bricks, square pens were constructed on the river bank to trap the silt. After two or three months this would be 'harvested', ground by a horse-driven mechanism and shaped into bricks for kiln-firing.

The bricks, some two or three inches across, were patented in 1827 by John Browne and became a world-wide commodity. They were given the name of Bath Brick since the colour after firing closely resembled that of Bath stone. At its peak, 24,000,000 bricks per year were being produced by ten different Bridgwater companies, especially during the First World War, when they were part of the soldier's standard kit issue. By the start of the Second World War they had been replaced by those tall cans of kitchen scourer.

Castle House

Apart from the conventional clay bricks with which Bridgwater is associated, cement blocks were also recognised as a building material. Castle House, in Queen Street, was built in 1851 as an example of how pre-cast concrete could be used as a building material. The company of Acremans acquired the local franchise for Portland Cement, the base material for the concrete blocks. With the Great Exhibition of 1851 imminent, the opportunity was grasped to demonstrate how Portland Cement products could be used and Castle House was created.

Visitors came in their hundreds from across the country, but the idea never really took off. Ahead of its time, concrete became the building material of choice in the 1950s, when some real monstrosities were built. Meanwhile, Castle House remains the first example in the world of a house built from pre-cast concrete, 100 years ahead of its time.

Allowed to fall into a state of disrepair, it became a target for vandals. The local authority appeared to be powerless to enforce any maintenance on the dwelling until the television programme *Restoration*, which sparked local interest and, at the time of writing, plans are afoot to bring about its long-awaited recovery.

Wicker products

Another one-time Bridgwater industry was basket-making using the local willows, or withies. The industry was active throughout the nineteenth and well into the twentieth centuries, with many small basket-making concerns based in private homes. The Second World War created a demand for wicker baskets, which were used for dropping supplies by parachute into enemy-occupied territory. The resilience and flexibility of the willow made these baskets ideal for the purpose. Laundry baskets, bicycle baskets, picnic hampers, fishing baskets, lobster pots and garden and household furniture were all made in the town.

Popular varieties of willow for the withy industry were Black Mole and Champion. Simply taking a cutting of a stem and pushing it into the clay soil was enough to propagate the plant. These were grown, and still are to a lesser extent, across the low-lying parts of Sedgemoor. While the willow growers worked in continually damp conditions, the work of the basket makers was at least in the dry. It was nonetheless back-aching work, sitting on the floor, back against the wall, with the basket being woven between the legs. Apart from the cottage industries, there were a number of manufacturing centres around the town: Squibs in Mount Street, Kraft Production in Cornboro Place, Betalls in West Street and Slocombe's in New Road.

✦ CHAPTER 8 ✦

The Early-Twentieth Century

The twentieth century for Bridgwater was dominated by matters both local and national. It was a century which saw two world wars, each of which left its mark on the town. It was also a century dominated by the decline of the docks and brick and tile trade and the rise and fall of the local Cellophane plant, which employed a high percentage of the local labour force. But we begin by taking a look at the first decade, before the advent of the First World War, a decade which saw the launch of the last Bridgwater-built ketch.

The Introduction of Electricity, 1903

In 1903 the Board of Trade granted a licence to the Bridgwater & District Electricity Supply & Traction Engine Co. to supply Bridgwater, Durleigh and Wembdon with electricity. The work, including digging up roads and railway, had to be completed within two years, and included the building of a generating station in Mount Street. The power came on supply in 1904, the last area of the town to have its gas lighting replaced being St Mary Street.

Amazingly it was gas that was used to generate the electricity. Only direct current was available and sold for 2d. a unit with a 4d. or 7d. tariff if used for lighting. In time the National Grid arrived, bringing the safer alternating current. This left consumers with the interim problem of using electrical items requiring one type of current whilst the available supply was of a different type.

The New Town Fire Stations, 1906 and 1964

The earliest reference to a fire engine in Bridgwater was in 1725, when the controversial George Bubb Doddington donated one to the town. In 1830 the engine, almost certainly not the 1725 version, was kept near the south gate. By 1880 the brigade was based around the back of the Town Hall in Clare Street, where a new fire station was built in 1906. At that time Bridgwater was much smaller than it is today. There was no significant housing beyond the railway line and no Hamp or Durleigh estates. The fire brigade was made up of volunteers who lived and worked near the town centre. When the alarm bell sounded they would run to the station, the first two to arrive dragging out the wheeled water pump and running with it to the fire, while the later arrivals would catch up on bicycles. On one occasion they were timed at eight minutes from arrival at the station to reaching the fire.

In 1935, life got easier when a petrol-driven engine arrived. In 1964 the brigade moved to its current headquarters in Colley Lane, after a short spell based at the cattle market in Bath Road.

The Launch of the *Irene* 1907

On the East Quay was once Carver's Yard, a shipbuilding yard complete with dry dock. It was here that the *Irene* was built and launched in 1907. She was especially designed to work the channel ports for the Colthurst & Symons Co. At the end of her

The launch of the Irene *in 1907 from Carver's Yard.*   (FROM THE ROGER EVANS COLLECTION)

days, left to decay, she was rescued and restored and served until just a few years ago, when an unfortunate fire almost destroyed her. At the time of writing, her future is uncertain.

The Tasmanian Flag, September 1910

The Empire Society, whose role it was to promote the British Empire, recognised that the younger generation had no awareness of what imperialism was all about. It appeared that when questioned as to the meaning of imperialism, the youngsters of Bridgewater, Tasmania, thought the word meant war. In order to promote a better understanding, it was decided that, around the commonwealth, schools would exchange flags with schoolchildren in towns of the same name.

The Union Flag was unfurled in Bridgewater, Tasmania, on Empire Day and then sent by the Tasmanian mayor, Edward S. Smithers, to the mayor of our Bridgwater. Eastover School, as the oldest state board school in the town, was chosen to be the recipient. Thus the flag was hoisted in the boys' playground, the words 'From the children of Bridgewater, Tasmania' having been added by the children of Mrs Rees's class at Eastover.

An Unwanted Suffragette, 1914

In June 1914 a young woman suspected of being a Suffragette stayed in the town, in accommodation in King Square. The police kept a vigilant eye on her, suspecting her of having an explosive device in the

The Union Flag from Tasmania is raised at Eastover School, 1910. (FROM THE ROGER EVANS COLLECTION)

Dorothy bag which she always carried. On one occasion she visited St Mary's Church, closely followed by the police inspector, who sat immediately behind her. Everyone in the church was aware of her presence and tension mounted as the service progressed. At the end of the service, the young woman picked up her bag and left town, never to return.

Hospital Saturday in 1910, a fund-raising event. (FROM THE ROGER EVANS COLLECTION)

The local Army Service Corps in 1914 marching to the railway station on their way to war.

(FROM THE ROGER EVANS COLLECTION)

The First World War

When the war against Germany was announced in 1914, there was a general feeling of euphoria. 'It'll all be over by Christmas' was the general belief and hundreds signed up to serve their country. Hundreds of Bridgwater men were destined never to return and their names, over 300 in total, are engraved on the war memorial in King Square.

So many men went to war that the immediate effect at home was that wages rose by a shilling a week. Wicker baskets, shirts and bandoliers for the fighting men took priority on the list of items produced locally. Those who went and fought were promised a 'land fit for heroes' on their return. But it was some while in coming. The centre of Bridgwater was packed with tiny cottages in tiny courts, where people lived in poverty. It was not until the late 1920s and 1930s that slum clearance began, the residents being rehoused on the Newtown estate and Taunton Road. Not many could afford the rents by then, however, one man in every three being unemployed.

West Street had the highest density of courts, with 17 in one street. Friarn Street and St John Street were similar. Narrow archways led into small, circular courtyards where two-up, two-down cottages clustered in the limited space. In the mid-nineteenth century these courtyards had been rife with cholera and in 1938 it was typhoid from which the residents suffered. Schools and public meeting places were closed. As the undertakers collected the bodies of those who died, so the mattresses and bedding were taken away for burning. It was the construction of the houses along Kidsbury Road in 1927 that heralded the introduction of decent housing.

The King Square war memorial.

(FROM THE ROGER EVANS COLLECTION)

Fore Street around 1910 (above) *and 1930* (below).   (FROM THE ROGER EVANS COLLECTION)

Fore Street with old charabancs. (FROM THE ROGER EVANS COLLECTION)

Changes in Transport

Perhaps the most significant change in the town came in the 1920s and 1930s, when motorised vehicles replaced horse-drawn carriages. By 1925 it was necessary to introduce Trinidadian asphalt and, later, tarmacadam. This, of course, brought an end to the Cornhill bonfire but greatly improved conditions for motorists and pedestrians alike. Amongst the earliest powered lorries were the steam-driven wagons of Peace's, whose premises were on the West Quay, and of the Gas Co., which used the new vehicle for hauling coke, one of which was driven by my wife's grandfather, Walter England, who lived in Kidsbury Road.

The Bridgwater Haulage Co. also had steam-driven lorries and caught the attention of the authorities in 1912 when an employee was fined 10s. for breaking the speed limit of two miles an hour.

The Bridgwater Pageant, 1927

Imagine the site where the Cellophane complex now stands and imagine it as open fields with a manor house at its centre. That is how it was in 1927, when an enormous pageant was held there to celebrate the town's history. The mayor of the town, Alderman Walter Deacon, had been inspired by a pageant held at Midelney Manor, near Hambridge, and felt it was appropriate to have one for Bridgwater. Concerned

Major Cely Trevilian, organiser of the 1927 Pageant.
(FROM THE ROGER EVANS COLLECTION)

The fair and funeral scenes from the pageant.   (FROM THE ROGER EVANS COLLECTION)

over the lack of local feeling for history and heritage, he recruited the services of Major Cely Trevilian, who had organised the Midelney Pageant. It was decided to hold the pageant, in June of 1927, to portray periods of the town's history and to develop a desire within performers and spectators alike to discover more. It turned out to be the biggest event to hit the town since the Monmouth Rebellion.

The sponsor of the event was Philip Sturdy, the owner of Sydenham Manor, where the pageant was held. He was quite a character himself and owned a car shaped like a boat, in which he would pass through the town each day as he headed via Durleigh Road over the hills to Taunton. The script was

written and a number of professionals recruited, although the majority of the 1,000 performers were local people. A 2,000-seat stand was built and tickets went on sale. It was a complete sell out. For the benefit of those who were unable to afford a ticket, a concession was made for them to view the rehearsals.

To ensure that everyone would understand what was being said, Mrs Norah Soole, an elocutionist, was brought in from Poole. Dressed as the Spirit of the Bridge, she introduced the scenes heralded by trumpeters of the 5th Somerset Light Infantry. She told the story of how the land around had been marshes, with a constant battle between the river and the sea. Groups of dancing girls melodramatically

The Blake (above left) *and Sedgemoor scenes* (above right) *, 1927.*   (FROM THE ROGER EVANS COLLECTION)

Massed performers (above) *and the procession through the town* (below).

(FROM THE ROGER EVANS COLLECTION)

rushed backwards and forwards, symbolising the waves. A family of lake dwellers entered and watched as land and sea battled against one another. Then there came a jester, whose role was to introduce each scene. First came King John, granting the town free borough status. Then came the riots of 1381, the funeral procession of Sir Hugh Luttrell (albeit it had little to do with Bridgwater) and St Matthew's fair.

There followed scenes from the two periods of conflict – Blake during the Civil War and the Battle of Sedgemoor.

For the climax of the show, the 1,000 performers all came together and, to the delight of the spectators, even marched in procession through the town. In the national press the event was declared an outstanding success.

Between the Wars

The 1930s proved a desperate time for the working community. In 1933 over 2,000 were unemployed in the town and massive queues formed around King Square leading to the Labour Exchange. Children scavenged around waste bins, looking for food and clothing. Three-quarters of the children in the town's six elementary schools were in rags with cardboard stuffed into their shoes. Despite their poverty, the children were well behaved, the cane still being in regular use. Child mortality levels were high, children's coffins being made of thin wood to keep down the cost. The presence of three pawnbrokers in the town centre reflected the dire needs of the townspeople: there was Best's at the Cornhill, Paul's in Eastover and Fred Evis in George Street, complete with the three balls of the pawnbroker over the doorway. It was not until 1955 that the latter finally closed down.

With unemployment high, Bridgwater was desperate to attract a major manufacturer and Courtaulds provided the solution. In 1934 the reservoir was opened at Ashford, and in 1938 the Durleigh Reservoir was opened. When the rest of the country was suffering from a drought, with water rationing, Bridgwater hit the headlines because it was one of the few towns not to be rationed. In their Coventry head office, the board members of Samuel Courtaulds were discussing where they could open the country's first production unit manufacturing the new commodity – 'Cellophane'. They needed a workforce of thousands, easy access to tidal waters to take away the effluent and a reliable supply of water. Their attention turned to Bridgwater and its reliable supply of water. That, combined with the tidal River Parrett and local unemployment running at around 30 per cent, was sufficient for them to open the plant which was to employ more than 2,500 employees in its heyday in the 1960s to 1980s. Inevitably, substitute products such as polypropylene diminished demand and the factory, which commenced production in 1938, finally closed in 2005, by which time the workforce was fewer than 250.

Meanwhile, the town remained a market town, although trade was outgrowing the limited space in the Penel Orlieu area where the cattle and pigs were sold. In 1935 the market was moved to its Bath Road site, where it remained in operation until the 1990s.

Some light relief came in 1937 with the coronation of King George VI, which was celebrated in style.

Above: *Cornhill celebrations.* Right: *Coronation programme, 1937.*
(FROM THE ROGER EVANS COLLECTION)

✦ CHAPTER 9 ✦

The Second World War

Vernon Bartlett

In September 1938 Neville Chamberlain was in Munich signing an agreement with Hitler and Mussolini. This was the 'Peace in our time' document, with which Chamberlain returned as a hero. Not everyone believed in the integrity of the agreement, however. Vernon Bartlett, a journalist and broadcaster with a Belgian wife, had seen at first hand what was happening in Europe and did not believe for one minute that Hitler's intentions were sincere. He wanted Parliament to understand that.

In November 1938, at a by-election in Bridgwater, Bartlett stood as an Independent candidate. His opponent was Patrick Heathcote-Amory, who expected an easy victory in a constituency which was rock-solid Tory. Bartlett's platform being a one-issue 'anti-Hitler' stand, the government did not want to see him win and use his position in Parliament to stir up the European issue. Bartlett won with a landslide and used his influence as an MP to challenge the Munich Agreement. He turned out to be the most respected MP the town had ever had.

As the autumn of 1939 approached, the nation was aware of the impending war. Those previously in the forces were called up as reservists and conscription was introduced. That July members of the Bridgwater ARP (Air Raid Precautions) brigade took part in their first full-scale practice. One Saturday night all lights were extinguished as shopkeepers, motorists and cyclists respected the blackout. Shortly before midnight the air-raid wardens waited at their posts. At their High Street headquarters, two first-aid parties, two immediate action parties and a decontamination unit set off in their lorries. The auxiliary fire brigade stood at the ready, with Boy Scouts acting as messengers. At midnight the wardens telephoned in their first prearranged reports of damage and injuries. A 'fire' at the Odeon required the fire brigade and the immediate action squad, first aiders took the walking wounded to the medical centre in Mount Street and the decontamination squad sorted out the 'gas attack' which had hit Castle Street. By one o'clock it was all over and by half past the ARPs had gone home, leaving the organisers to review the successes and failures of the exercise.

The Day War Broke Out

'This country is now at war with Germany. We are ready.' The nation heard the Prime Minister's words over their wireless sets on 3 September 1939. Across the town were distributed gas masks, to be carried at all times. The *Bridgwater Mercury* for 6 September carried an article on the king's speech and on the need for 'Somerset homes for mothers and children'. As the men of the town were called up and headed away, many never to return, evacuees from London began to arrive. Across the nation, three million women and children were on the move. Bridgwater took nearly 6,500, more than 1,000 in the first week who were to be housed in the town, with a further 1,000 destined for the villages, those from the East End of London arriving first.

It was tough on those children who arrived at Bridgwater railway station, confused and afraid, with luggage labels tied to their lapels bearing their identity. In many cases brothers and sisters were separated. The evacuees also brought scabies, ringworm and other complaints to the town. It was 8 September when the first two trainloads arrived with their teachers and were marched down to St John's School. There they were given biscuits, chocolate and a tin of meat before being allocated to a family by the billeting officer, Mr P.H. Beckett. Then, for those destined for the villages, it was on to a fleet of motor buses. That same evening a further 800 arrived and were taken to Eastover School for processing. On the Saturday and Sunday yet more refugees arrived, and were still coming late on Monday evening, by which time the billeting officer had finished for the day.

Parents were free to visit their children whenever they could – but it was very difficult with London being bombed and travel restricted. When they arrived it was no better. In case of a German invasion, all place names and direction signs had been removed and the Eastenders found it daunting getting to the local villages. The cultural shock of moving from the bustling street life of London to rural Somerset proved traumatic for many children and so the local Labour party opened up 27 Friarn Street as a community centre for the evacuees and their mothers. A hostel was built at Sunnybank, off Rhode Lane, for the same purpose. By June of 1940 they were still arriving, a further 750 in that month alone. Once again, Eastover School was their first point of call, where a medical and a bottle of milk preceded their transfer to new homes.

Many evacuee children ended up at Wembdon, where the school and church, their windows covered with wire mesh, had been identified as the places to

Bridgwater Town Council promoted 'Veg for Victory'.

go in case of an air raid. In all, 123 children were allocated to the school and 25 to the church. On 27 September 1940 the air-raid siren sounded and a German Junkers dropped its load of bombs over Wembdon, a mere quarter of a mile from the school and church. It was a lucky escape. The following month, only 140 more evacuees arrived – the pace was slowing and Bridgwater was coming to terms with the mini-invasion.

Rationing and Restrictions

Life was changing rapidly. Food shortages and rationing, the disappearance of the menfolk and the blackouts soon led to the cancellation of all kinds of events, even the town's carnival procession. Bridgwater Fair turned up with just one motorcycle show and one set of dodgems, and by 7p.m. it was 'all lights out'.

The blackout was taken very seriously. One chink of light could be all it took to attract the attentions of a German bomber. The *Bridgwater Mercury* each week published the blackout times. The lack of lighting had its humorous side. My mother was a wartime postwoman. In the early hours of the morning, in total darkness, she would cycle to the Post Office with just a narrow slit showing of her front light. Each morning she would pass a policeman on his way to work. 'Morning, Postie!' he would say, to which she replied, "Morning, Bobbie!" – neither having a clue as to who the other person was. Gleaning the pages of the *Mercury* for those war years it was obvious that accidents and fatalities increased significantly during blackout hours, including people falling into the river or docks.

Some businesses did well out of the war. Those selling material for blackout curtains, heavy tape for windows in case of bomb blast, clothing, food and bedding for evacuees, all did well. Even the *Mercury* advertised: 'Minimise loss of trade through darkened windows by displaying your goods in the columns of this newspaper.' British Cellophane was well promoted in an advertisement which gave details of how Cellophane could be glued to windows to prevent blast damage, even providing the recipe for making the glue. A house on the corner of North Street and Penel Orlieu was used as a show house for this and various other safety ideas.

Throughout the war, food, petrol, clothing and many other essentials were in short supply. Rationing was introduced and the nation encouraged to 'Dig for Victory'. By 1943 600 new allotments had been created and breeding rabbits for meat and keeping chickens were common practices. Hoarding became an issue which was discouraged by the government and promoted by the shopkeepers.

Casualties

The initial 'buzz' after the outbreak of war turned to concern and sadness as news came through of fatalities overseas. Everyone dreaded the arrival of the young telegram boy bearing the message from the Ministry of War. Two weeks into the war, the *Mercury* reported the loss of the aircraft carrier HMS *Courageous* with 500 men. Charles Wood of Cecil Terrace, one of the survivors, had clung to a piece of timber for an hour before being picked up. Cecil James, who worked at the Van Heusen shirt factory before the war, was one of four Bridgwater men to go

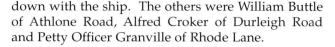

down with the ship. The others were William Buttle of Athlone Road, Alfred Croker of Durleigh Road and Petty Officer Granville of Rhode Lane.

Prisoners of War

After the loss of the *Courageous*, the news dried up. Papers were censored and the reporting of losses was banned. The war memorial in King Square tells the story of the many lives lost in that period of conflict. Likewise, there were many who were taken prisoner. One example was Ron Authers, who was captured at the fall of Singapore and spent the remainder of the war as a prisoner of war of the Japanese, suffering the tortures of the camps on the 'Railway of Death' and the Bridge on the River Kwai. His is an amazing story, told in *Somerset's Forgotten Heroes*.

At home German and Italian POWs began to appear in the town. Germans were kept at a camp in Colley Lane and Italians at Goathurst, all living in new huts and reasonably well looked after, with about 500 men in each camp. In return for their good care they were employed, mostly in agricultural work, and could be seen walking freely around the town with yellow patches on their backs. Fraternisation with the local community certainly took place and there are many Bridgwater folk alive today who prefer not to talk about the socialising of certain local girls with those captured members of the enemy forces.

The Women's Land Army and the War Effort

For the ladies, the war brought fresh opportunities with the demand for war work. For those with secretarial skills, there was work to be done at army bases. With local factories turned over to the war effort, many housewives took jobs there, while others joined the Women's Land Army, using and repairing tractors and working in the fields.

The local Cellophane plant produced film capable of protecting ammunition from the humid climate of the Far East. In the engineering department sections were made for the Mulberry Harbour which would prove so critical on D-Day. Landing craft were manufactured by Light Buoyant at Saltlands. The Trojan Works (later the site of Wellworthy and then Bordens) made shell cases. Wicker baskets, used for dropping supplies by parachute, were made all over town and, of course, high explosives were produced at the Royal Ordnance Factory. The Electro-Dynamic Construction Co. in Bristol Road made electric motors for tanks and aircraft.

Air Raids

The first hint of an air raid on Bridgwater came on 1 August 1940, when a Heinkel HEIII dropped a land-mine at Bankland Farm, Northmoor, leaving a huge crater. The crater still exists and has created a pond large enough for swans to nest there. Nearby, an unexploded magnetic mine required the attentions of the bomb disposal brigade from Devonport. The impact of this explosion was felt in Bridgwater, although no damage was done. Two weeks later, in a small air battle over Puriton Hill, a Heinkel was shot down. The five German aircrew parachuted to safety except for one, who was shot and wounded on the way down. They were all captured and taken into Bridgwater.

Later that month, on 24/25 August, Bridgwater was visited by a German raider who, we must assume, had failed to find his intended target and was flying home over Bridgwater when he released around 200 incendiaries which landed across Cranleigh Gardens and the brickyard at Colley Lane. The aircraft then dropped heavy bombs over Southgate Terrace in Old Taunton Road, where six houses were damaged, three more destroyed and seven people killed. Daisy Balham was killed by the blast and her body was found still seated on her chair in the cupboard under the stairs, bag of runner beans in one hand and paring knife in the other. ARP Warden Len Wilkins, woken by the alarm signal, was putting his boots on when he was killed instantly, along with his wife Gladys and thirteen-year-old daughter Margaret. A Mr and Mrs Collard were also killed. One unlucky brickyard worker had actually been told to go into his home, where he was killed, for his own safety. The colleague who had given him that advice was later to drag his body from the debris.

Lucky survivors included a 100-year-old parrot which never spoke again and an eight-year-old boy who woke in bed screaming that he was on fire. His mother and grandmother dragged him from the room and threw bucketfuls of water onto the burning bed. Mac Hawkins, in his book *Somerset at War*, tells the lovely story of Harry Rainey who, on the night of that raid, shouted for his wife to hurry up and get into their Anderson air-raid shelter. 'Me teeth… Me teeth… I can't find me teeth,' she shouted. Harry bellowed back, 'Don't worry about them, maid – they's chuckin' bombs, not bloody sandwiches!' Following the devastation in Old Taunton Road, the council agreed that 20 air raid shelters should be built around the town. Members of the public were meanwhile building Anderson-style shelters in their own back gardens. Bill Holland, of Chilton Street, remembers how his father, a railway employee, built a shelter in their garden from railway sleepers, which was stocked by his mother with emergency rations.

The next raid to come was that by a single Junkers in the early morning of 1 October 1940. Having flown over the town, it released its high-explosive load harmlessly on Geoff Moate's farm near Kidsbury Road, one bomb failing to explode. Later that day, a British plane crashed at Cockerhurst Farm at Wembdon, when a balloon cable-cutting experiment went badly wrong. It appears the photographer leaned too far out of the plane and managed to entangle himself in the control wires of the cutting equipment. The pilot survived, having parachuted out, but the photographer, Mr R.O. Tipple was killed. The Royal Aircraft Establishment had a huge hangar for balloons at Pawlett and it was from here that the trials were being conducted. The intention was to discover a way for British pilots to safely negotiate their way through enemy balloon barrages.

Much damage was caused around the town when two magnetic mines exploded on the night of 20 March 1941. They fell relatively harmlessly in the Meads, near the Fairfield, but such was the impact from the blast that nearly 1,500 premises around the town centre had windows blown out and one person was killed. Incendiaries were also dropped and a young Dennis Searle, co-grandfather to two of my granddaughters, told of how he found one stuck in the bank of Durleigh Brook. He took it home as a souvenir and hid it under his sister's bed. There it was discovered by his father, who placed it in a carrier bag and cycled it down to the police station, the bag swinging from the handlebars of his bike.

In October 1941 a German plane was shot down over Wembdon and the pilot killed. His uniform was recovered and somehow ended up on display in the window of the Bridgwater Gas Co., along with parts of the plane, arrows pointing to the blood of the dead German officer. Mary Walbridge, realising what was going on, gave vent to her anger, pointing out that he may have been the enemy, but he was still a mother's son. The next raid came in February 1942, when a British aircrew on an exercise accidentally dropped their payload on East Brent, Bridgwater and Woolavington.

Bridgwater was fortunate in that it suffered few raids compared to other Somerset centres, Bath in particular, which suffered terribly in the Baedeker raids. The ARP records for the duration indicate a total of 263 high explosive bombs, 6,671 incendiaries, two oil bombs, 10 land and other mines, 63 unexploded bombs, 1,638 buildings damaged and four enemy aircraft shot down. All of this came in the Bridgwater area.

The GIs Arrive

In 1943 American forces appeared in Bridgwater and across the country, many of them billeted in homes providing a bed but not meals, for which the householder received 10d. a day – British servicemen were only worth 6d. a day. In the main the Americans were welcomed, especially by the ladies, less so by the men, many of whom regarded them as an 'invasion force'. Dances were arranged for them at the Blake Hall and at such local factories as British

Cellophane. The YMCA, Blake Hall and Cranleigh Gardens Annexe acted as canteens. At a British Cellophane dance, the factory ladies who turned up were taken aback to find a negro contingent in attendance. It took one brave lady to cross the dance floor before the ice was broken. Black American troops were not allowed to fraternise with white women, and even consensual sex with a white woman, considered to be statutory rape, under American law carried the death penalty. One black GI was executed at Shepton Mallet gaol for liaising with a white English woman, although there was no rape as we define it. In all, 21 GIs were hanged at Shepton Mallet and two executed by firing squad. These latter being Native Americans, death by hanging was against their religion.

More American servicemen arrived in 1944, when the Westonzoyland aerodrome was turned over to 9th Troop Carrier Command, previously used to train British pilots. Their main objective was to provide a glider squadron in readiness for the D-Day landings. They made an awesome sight as they flew over the town en masse towing their gliders. On D-Day they departed and their places were taken by 422nd Troop Carrier Command paratroopers, who flew out in the days that followed. At the end of the war, many were sad to see the Americans go and some even went with them. Carol Chapman and Rene Cornish, both from Athlone Road, were among those who left for a life overseas.

The Home Guard

The Home Guard, or Local Defence Volunteers, was set up in May 1940 to protect against enemy invaders. Bridgwater had its own unit, the 10th Somerset Battalion, under the command of Lt-Col R. Chamberlain, based at the Drill Hall and manned by 2,500 men split into platoons. The Cellophane plant had its own, No. 5 Platoon, while No. 6 Platoon was reserved for railwaymen, with a particular requirement to defend the Somerset Bridge. Initially they were armed only with pick-axe handles and an arm band labelled LDV. Then Lord Wharton, from Goathurst, supplied them with a couple of double-barrelled shotguns of which, within a week, one had been dropped and broken. Eventually uniforms, arms and other kit arrived and the LDV looked a more serious unit. Three years later, they even had grenades and many a Bridgwater home had a rifle in the corner of the front room.

Number 6 platoon drilled regularly in the grounds of Eastover School, next to the railway. On an exercise in which they combined with the Cellophane contingent, a misdirected smoke grenade brought a straight-through passenger train to an unexpected stop. At the back of the railway station was a spigot mortar gun emplacement. On an exercise which took advantage of a Scottish regiment conveniently in the area, a thunderflash lobbed in the emplacement set fire to the seat of the trousers of one of the LDV lads, who promptly resigned. The Scots also managed to blow out several windows in Devonshire Street, where a freshly painted house had to be repainted.

Membership of the LDV was, in some cases, compulsory and Wilf Palmer, who worked for Hancock's, the scrap metal dealer, was given a three-month prison sentence with hard labour for refusing to join.

Other forms of defence were the searchlight positions – one at Sutton Mallet, another on Wembdon Hill – and the Q stations, identified as QF or QL sites, the F being for fire and the L for lighting. These were decoy sites and the nearest was on Pendon Hill at Stawell, where lighting was set up in imitation of a factory to confuse enemy bombers at night. Immediately it was calculated that the bomber observer had spotted them, the lights would be switched off, as would happen with a real factory. It was hoped that this ploy would draw enemy aircraft away from the ROF and Cellophane factories, as well as from Westonzoyland aerodrome. If bombs actually hit the site, barrels of fuel could be ignited to complete the illusion and keep the aircraft's attention, Stawell being both a QF and QL site.

Returning Heroes

As the war approached its end, so British POWs were being released and returned home. Henry Webber of Bath Road, Fred Hayman of Ashleigh Avenue and John Kerslake of North Street were Royal Marines captured at Tobruk and released as part of an exchange programme in 1943. Fred Edney of Gloucester Road and Donald Hill of Taunton Road, paratroopers captured at Arnhem, were in Stalag 11B with Bob Goodenough, also of Bridgwater. They never got to meet Norman Finch of the Cornhill, however, who escaped en route to the camp and made his way back home. From the Far East came Ron Authers, who had suffered in the Japanese camps at the Bridge on the River Kwai and was in Nagasaki when the atomic bomb was dropped there. It was the Far East POWs who had most visibly altered on their return. These men were just a few of the many.

Scores of Bridgwater men were to receive awards for their courage. The Distinguished Flying Cross was awarded to Cellophane's Billy Hill, Brendan Baker of Camden Road, who worked for the accountants Sellick & Dimmock, and Robert Hooper of Northfields. The British Empire Medal went to John Coles of Kingscliffe Terrace, Taunton Road, who worked for Thompson's the ironmongers, for dealing with unsafe explosives at sea. Clifford Searle, president in 2005 of our local YMCA, was awarded the Distinguished Conduct Medal for bravery in Italy, where he served as a commando. His story is told in *Forgotten Heroes of Bridgwater*. There were, of course, others, many of whom did not wish their name to be mentioned here.

VE Day

Victory finally came with the fall of Germany and the nation celebrated. The town took on festive garb, decked in bunting and banners. Fireworks, dances and kisses on the Cornhill went on well beyond midnight. Flags hung from every window and the Cornhill dome was coloured red, white and blue. The celebrations, which continued for two solid days, culminated in a bonfire on the Fairfield. The blackouts were discarded, the church bells rang, ships' hooters sounded in the dock and trains blew their whistles. The carnival committee announced that they were back in business. Within months, victory in the Far East was also won and the boys began to return home.

Bridgwater Home Guard, No. 3 Platoon.   (FROM THE ROGER EVANS COLLECTION)

The author in 1948, sitting on the knee of the moustached Gerald Wills, Bridgwater's MP, at an occasion promoting National Health orange juice. My mother is immediately behind the MP.
(FROM THE ROGER EVANS COLLECTION)

Above: *The Branksome Avenue coronation street party. The author is the lad on the left, immediately behind the cake. The picture includes the Atyeo, Elson, Evans, Griffiths, Manley, Morris and Pratt families.* (FROM THE ROGER EVANS COLLECTION)

Right: *The programme of Bridgwater's coronation celebrations.*
(FROM THE ROGER EVANS COLLECTION)

BRIDGWATER
CORONATION CELEBRATIONS
JUNE, 1953
OFFICIAL SOUVENIR PROGRAMME   PRICE 6d.

CHAPTER 10

Postwar Bridgwater

Bridgwater Carnival

It would be impossible to write a book on the history of Bridgwater and not include the world-famous Bridgwater Carnival. However, having recently published *Somerset Carnivals*, in which the history and origins of Bridgwater Carnival are covered in detail, I do not wish to duplicate the information here and shall deal with the subject of carnival only briefly.

It all began, of course, in 1605, with the gunpowder plot, though in fact the associated bonfire celebrations date back much earlier, even to pagan times. In Bridgwater the propensity of public houses in the town centre was sufficient to create a competitive atmosphere when it came to the making of guys to go on the bonfire. Thus the guys became bigger and better and someone eventually came up with the idea that they should be fancy dressed, and that it was permissible to enter more than one in the competition, at which point a farm cart was needed to display them. When those who produced the guys dressed up and sang and danced around the carts carrying the still-life dummies, the carnival as we know it today was born, albeit tractors have replaced horses, generators have replaced paraffin lamps and everything is on an astronomical scale compared to those original processions.

Key dates in the history of the carnival are: 1881, when a formal committee was created; 1883, when the first carnival concert was held; and 1924, when the last bonfire on the Cornhill was lit.

Industrial Growth and Decline

The second half of the twentieth century has seen a more rapid change in the manufacturing base than at any other period. The wicker works are gone and the brickyards have closed, the last of these, Barham's, firing the kiln for the last time in 1965. The Somerset & Dorset Railway closed its Bridgwater links in 1952, when passenger traffic came to an end. Starkey, Knight & Ford closed their Northgate brewery in 1964, which was also the year that traffic wardens arrived. In 1971 the docks closed. It was also in this period that, in 1974, the old Bridgwater Borough Council disappeared under local government reorganisation.

It was a period during which the Cellophane plant went into decline, especially in the 1980s and

The Northgate Brewery in 1865. (FROM THE BRIDGWATER TOWN COUNCIL COLLECTION, COURTESY THE BLAKE MUSEUM)

The popular Bridgwater Lido.   (COURTESY KEITH PAINTER)

1990s, during which time the workforce declined from 2,500 to 250. At the same time new businesses came to the town. Bonded Fibre Fabrics opened in 1951 and the Quantock Preserving Co., now Gerber Foods, has seen huge growth. Undoubtedly there were many businesses which stayed away from the town, taking their manufacturing bases elsewhere, because of the 'Bridgwater smell'. Hopefully the recent closure of the Cellophane plant will bring its own silver lining as businesses prove less reluctant to base themselves here.

Life Goes On

Amidst all this change, life goes on. One feature of those postwar years was the baby boom. I was one of them, arriving in 1947. In those years rationing still applied but the government was concerned about the health of its children. Consequently, orange juice was supplied through Down House, the Social Services centre in Eastover, and all primary schoolchildren received their one-third of a pint of school milk, which came in glass bottles and had to be thawed out on the classroom stove during the winter months.

The king died in 1952 and the nation celebrated the Coronation of Her Majesty Queen Elizabeth II in June 1953. Across the town, street parties were held.

The town was becoming busier, especially with the spread of motor cars which, although they had been around for decades, had yet to reach the huge numbers we see today. Traffic was sufficient by the 1950s, however, that the town had become known as the 'Bottleneck on the A38', and holiday traffic would queue for miles as it tried to pass through the town. It should be remembered that at that time there was no motorway and only one road bridge over the river. Everything went through Eastover and Fore Street. A second bridge having become a necessity, in 1957 the Blake Bridge opened, the dual carriageway of Broadway taking traffic away from the town centre.

The extension of Broadway beyond Taunton Road to North Street resulted in the demolition of one end of Friarn Street but permitted access to the land which was to become the new Bridgwater Lido, a new, improved open-air swimming pool which opened in 1960, replacing its dilapidated predecessor in Old Taunton Road. Perhaps the new pool was a lot larger than the old and perhaps it was pure coincidence, but the following year the town was hit by severe water shortages and water-supplies were switched off throughout the daylight hours. When the lido closed it was replaced by the less popular, albeit indoor, Sedgemoor Splash.

Preparatory work on the new Blake Bridge, 1956.

The Cannon junction, where the Bristol and Bath Roads meet, 1905.

CHAPTER 11

Around and About the East Side

It is easy to state that Bridgwater has changed much in recent years, with new bridges across the river and huge housing estates, supermarkets and industrial estates springing up. And yet much of the town remains as it was 800 years ago. The shape of the town centre, if not its appearance, remains fundamentally unaltered.

The length of the street called Eastover remains unchanged. At the eastern end, by the Cobblestones public house, stood the gated entrance to the town. Fore Street, St Mary Street, the High Street, Dampiet Street, Binford Place, King Street, Blake Street, Friarn Street, Horsepond Lane and Penel Orlieu remain unaltered in their fundamental layout. On the eastern side of the town, it was only after 1841 that any development took place beyond the end of Eastover. St John Street and Wellington Road were all built in around the 1840s. Terraced houses were erected in Bristol Road and Monmouth Street in 1851, Devonshire Street was built in 1869 and Edward Street in 1880.

In this chapter the intention is to pick up on those odd interesting facts which failed to fit in naturally elsewhere. If a particular place is not mentioned in this section the reader should look for it in earlier chapters.

One feature of the townscape now missing is that of the many old pubs which the town once boasted. That particular subject justifying a volume in its own right, it is recommended that the reader dip into David Williams's publication, *Bridgwater Inns Past and Present*.

The Cannon

Take a visit to the Bristol Road cemetery and, as you walk along the path leading down through the graves, there in the top right-hand corner of the field is a white marble cross with the inscription *Erected by Friends to Commemorate One of the Gallant Six Hundred.* This is the last resting place of Denis Heron, who once lived on the Salmon Parade, near the hospital. His fascinating story is fully described in *The Forgotten Heroes of Bridgwater* and *Somerset's Forgotten Heroes.* Suffice it here to say that he rode with the 4th Light Dragoons in the historic Charge of the Light Brigade.

To celebrate the presence of this hero in the town, in 1857, three years after the charge, the borough council petitioned Parliament for the provision of a Russian cannon, captured in the Crimea. The petition was granted and, when the gun arrived, it was accompanied by bands and a procession to its position outside Denis Heron's house, between the Town Bridge and the hospital, 40 yards from the bridge. The following year Denis retired but kept up his military duties as a Sergeant-Major in the West Somerset Yeomanry Cavalry, Bridgwater's own regiment. On his retirement from the Yeomanry, he took up employment with Sutton & Co., a Bridgwater firm, until his death at the age of 65.

The year of his retirement, 1883, was the year the new Town Bridge was opened. At the same time the cannon was moved from the Town Bridge to the junction of the Bath and Bristol Roads, a junction which thenceforth became known as 'The Cannon'. The gun was eventually taken for scrap for the war effort. In more recent years a replica cannon has been installed on the same spot, a timely reminder of a forgotten hero.

Imagine a time when there was no Bristol Road, when there was only the road to Bath. This was much narrower then and across it was a barrier, a swinging gate, where tolls were collected, and which was positioned more or less where the Hamlins premises are at the time of writing. The Great Western Railway branch line to the docks also once crossed this road. An old shunter, No. 1338, would cross several times a day, and the engine driver would allow children to ride on the footplate, a practice which carried on into the early 1960s. In those days, when there was no roundabout and the rail track crossed a wide expanse of road, level-crossing gates were rendered impractical and a railway employee would walk in front of the train holding a red warning flag.

Cranleigh Gardens and Eastover Park

Popularly called 'the rec', Cranleigh Gardens has a Victorian feel thanks to its avenues of horse chestnut trees. The bowling club and tennis-courts are well-used facilities, as is the Cranleigh Gardens Annexe. Built as an entertainment centre for the American forces, it now serves as a fitness centre. The park once had its own bandstand and an informal zoo featuring the local squirrels.

Running off Cranleigh Gardens is Gordon Terrace, where the town's first Roman Catholic church was built in 1846. It later served as a workshop for the Cummings family, who built farm carts and hay wagons here.

Eastover looking toward the town bridge. The Commercial Hotel, now the Cobblestones, is on the right, with the Queen's Head on the left. (FROM THE BRIDGWATER TOWN COUNCIL COLLECTION, COURTESY THE BLAKE MUSEUM)

Eastover

The name Eastover derives from the Saxon for east bank, *est ufer*, and although it now refers to a single street, historically it referred to the whole area east of the river but within the bounds of the town.

Troubles at the White Hart Inn

The White Hart Inn in Eastover is perhaps the longest operating premises in the street, dating back a few hundred years to when it was a coaching inn. The one-time landlady, Mrs Francis, kept a pet fox to help with the cooking. She cooked her meats on a spit, using a caged wheel to turn it – a bit like a large hamster play-wheel. She would put her pet fox into the wheel, which was guarded from the heat of the fire, and let the fox run and run, turning the spit.

One day the fox escaped and headed to Westonzoyland, where it became a nuisance, killing the local chickens. A Mr Portman from North Petherton was called in with his pack of foxhounds and chased the fox out to Athelney, then to Enmore,

The Ivorex plaque depicting the scene at the White Hart Inn. (FROM THE ROGER EVANS COLLECTION)

Mills Store at the junction of Church Street and Eastover. (COURTESY CHRIS HOCKING)

across to North Petherton and back into Bridgwater. Realising where it was, the fox headed straight for its home at the White Hart Inn, where it rushed through the petticoats of its mistress into the inn, jumped up into the spit-wheel and recommenced its culinary duties. Meanwhile, at the end of a 30-mile chase, Mr Portman's hounds tore into the inn to be met by Mrs Francis's wide-spread petticoats, which formed suffi-cient barrier to keep the hounds at bay until their master arrived to whip them off.

A few years ago I was lucky enough to meet a Westonzoyland lady whose lounge wall carried an Ivorex plaque. It was made by Arthur Osborne of Faversham in Kent, portraying this apparently true story.

Another troubled day at the White Hart Inn came in 1850, when political feelings were running high and the White Hart Inn was the home of the local Tories. Outside stood a band of Whigs, furious at the election results and ready for an argument. Tempers flared and the Tories hurled skittle pins and balls through the windows, targeting the Whigs, who hurled cobblestones and bricks in the opposite direc-tion. The fracas came to an end when the mayor read the Riot Act and declared martial law.

The Rex Cinema
Opposite the White Hart Inn, where the shop fronts are set well back from the kerb, there was once a group of shops known as the Arcade. In 1929 a cinema opened here which took the same name. Suffering a poor reputation, it was subject to a change of ownership and of name, becoming The Rex, popularly known as the Bug House or Flea Pit,

which is how most older members of the Bridgwater community remember it. It closed in 1956.

George Williams Memorial Hall – the YMCA
The YMCA was established in Bridgwater in 1850 and, in 1887, the Memorial Hall on the corner of Eastover was built in memory of its founder. In 1875 the Globe Hotel had been destroyed by fire and was pulled down, leaving the site clear for the develop-ment of the George Williams Memorial Hall. This magnificent building was allowed to fall into a state of disrepair and it was Bridgwater's loss when it was demolished. Near the YMCA were three small river-side buildings. One was a weighbridge, manned by Mr Pitman and then by Bert Brown. The others were toilets and a boot and shoe repairer. There was also a harbour master's office here, manned by Captain Charlie Smith, which disappeared when the river bank gave way in 1945 and it fell into the river.

East Quay

The older buildings along the quayside were formerly a warehouse, a temperance hotel and a Post Office, the latter featuring a wall clock used by travellers returning from London to correct their watch-pieces. What remained of Carver's boatyard was filled in in 1960, after a young lad fell in and drowned in the waterlogged basin.

Monmouth Street

Inventor of the Mackintosh
John Clark (1785–1853) was a local Quaker, born in

115

The Queen's Head Hotel in Eastover, 1865, demolished to make way for Broadway.

(FROM THE BRIDGWATER TOWN COUNCIL COLLECTION, COURTESY THE BLAKE MUSEUM)

Eastover, showing the Devonshire Arms and Bouchiers, 1904.

(FROM THE ROGER EVANS COLLECTION)

The fire-ruined Globe Hotel in Eastover, 1875.

(FROM THE BRIDGWATER TOWN COUNCIL COLLECTION, COURTESY THE BLAKE MUSEUM)

Eastover from the Town Bridge, c.1912.   (FROM THE ROGER EVANS COLLECTION)

East Quay in 1865, with a horse and cart waiting outside the Post Office.
(FROM THE BRIDGWATER TOWN COUNCIL COLLECTION, COURTESY THE BLAKE MUSEUM)

Above: *Mills the drapers in Monmouth Street, c.1900.*

Left: *Mills with* (left to right) *Bert M., H.J.C. and Reginald Mills.*

(COURTESY CHRIS HOCKING)

John Clark's Eureka machine.
(FROM THE ROGER EVANS COLLECTION)

Greinton, who moved to Bridgwater with his parents in 1809. An early career as a grocer was a disaster, and then he also failed as a painter before turning his hand to being an inventor. A cousin of Cyrus and James Clark, of the shoe dynasty, he developed a machine which took him 13 years to perfect. It contained a number of revolving wheels with letters on them. The wheels could be made to spin around, a bit like a fruit machine and, when they stopped, there would be a row of letters, but not quite at random. Clark had engineered the machine so that, no matter how the wheels spun, they would finish up spelling a sentence in Latin hexameter. Now if that leaves you wandering what a hexameter is, the dictionary defines it as:

A verse of six metrical feet where the first four are usually dactyls or spondees, the fifth almost always a dactyl, and the sixth a spondee or trochee.

If that leaves you as confused as it does me, it was simply a style of writing Greek or Roman epic poetry using six words per line. The idea was thus to create these lines and write them down until there were enough to string together into sextuplets. Called the Eureka, the machine can still be viewed in Clark's

shoe museum in Street. When it was exhibited in London, in 1845, the proceeds from the admission charges were sufficient for John Clark to buy himself a house in Monmouth Street which, at the time of writing, is next to Hamlin's garage.

Imagine how Clark's wife must have felt when, after 13 years, her husband had created a machine which produced Latin hexameter phrases. How she must have longed for him to produce something more practical. Returning home one day, soaked to the skin by a shower of rain, she suggested to her husband that his time might be more usefully spent inventing a waterproof material for clothing that could be worn in the rain. Clark worked on the idea and developed a technique for treating fabric so that it became waterproof. Numerous trials having proved totally successful, he patented the idea and then sold the patent to a man called Mackintosh for the sum of £40. The rest is history. Mackintosh became a household name for raincoats and the name of Clark remained associated with shoes.
Locally this eccentrically dressed inventor was nick-named 'First Mate from Noah's Ark'.

Salmon Parade

Once called Salmon Lane, this riverside road is dominated by the town's hospital, but between it and the bridge is an interesting row of former fishermen's cottages. Salmon was once one of the main catches here and, whilst it may seem amazing that salmon should ever have run in such a river, even in my childhood I would watch as they ran upstream. Pollution has presumably brought to an end what was once a good source of revenue. Their decline began in the 1930s, almost certainly with the opening of the local Cellophane plant, but at one time as many as 20 men were licensed to fish the river for salmon.

In 1803 the Revd William Holland, in diaries published under the title *Paupers and Pig Killers*, referred to the price of Bridgwater salmon having risen from 4d. a pound to 2s. – presumably a reflection of the end of the season producing fewer catches. Bill Pocock, a well-known local figure whose Uncle Ted worked on the coal barges, lived in one of the Salmon Parade cottages. Outside his cottage, when the season was right, there would be buckets full of mussels for sale.

Bill fished the river using a dip net. Sitting in his rowing boat, he would watch as the salmon rose, gasping for air in the silt-filled waters. Then, with the prowess of a dart player, he would throw a small piece of wood into the centre of the rings left by the rising fish. Next, he would row about 10ft upstream to where the salmon would next rise and stand poised at the rear of his boat, ready with his dip net to catch the rising fish. Although he was licensed, he still ended up in court. His licence dictated that he could take no more than six fish a day from Monday

Salmon Parade with fishermen's boats outside the hospital, c.1910.

The weighbridge and toilets (right) on Salmon Parade.

(FROM THE BRIDGWATER TOWN COUNCIL COLLECTION, COURTESY THE BLAKE MUSEUM)

Evans's store at the corner of Monmouth Street and St John Street.
(FROM THE BRIDGWATER TOWN COUNCIL COLLECTION, COURTESY THE BLAKE MUSEUM)

Evans's garage in St John Street – in 2006 the premises of Byron Wynn.
(FROM THE BRIDGWATER TOWN COUNCIL COLLECTION, COURTESY THE BLAKE MUSEUM)

to Saturday. He took eight fish on a Sunday and was prosecuted. His defence was that he was only limited on the number of fish he could take on the six days mentioned, no limit having been set for Sundays. He got off on a technicality but was warned not to try it again. Even the landlord of the River Parrett Inn, once called the Salmon Inn, was prosecuted for taking a salmon without a licence. The judge let him off, declaring it to be a sporting gesture.

Eels were another source of food in plentiful supply in the River Parrett and in June 1859 a sturgeon was caught weighing 160lbs which was sold at market at 6d. per pound. In 1913 a 168lb porpoise was caught in Bridgwater by Henry Laver.

Bridgwater Infirmary

Bridgwater expanded and became increasingly industrialised throughout the nineteenth century. Inevitably, such a town required its own hospital, and that which stands on Salmon Parade dates back to 1813, when a hospital was started in Back Street, now called Clare Street, roughly behind the present Town Hall. By 1820 demand had outstripped the capability of the premises and the hospital as we

Bridgwater Infirmary, 1865.   (FROM THE BRIDGWATER TOWN COUNCIL COLLECTION, COURTESY THE BLAKE MUSEUM)

know it today was purchased for £700 from public subscription. Each subscriber, providing £1 per year, could recommend four outpatients or their equivalents, one inpatient being worth two outpatients. Each inpatient then had to pay 5s.6d. per week. By 1830 the rules had changed to cater for longer-term patients. After three months as an inpatient, a fresh recommendation was required and each patient was required to pay one month's board in advance. They were also required to supply their own linen and bedside requirements.

The hospital grew from then until the end of the nineteenth century. In 1837 two new wards were added, a female ward was introduced in 1847 and in 1876 the frontage was altered to add the present portico. A new operating theatre was added in 1902, along with X-ray equipment. At the time of writing proposals are afoot for a brand new hospital.

There were other hospitals. In 1840 there was an eye infirmary in Victoria Street and in 1872 an infectious diseases hospital was opened. In Castle Street the Mary Stanley maternity unit, where the majority of Bridgwater's adult population were born, the author and his family included, existed for many years.

Sydenham Manor

Sydenham Manor, which still remains Bridgwater's best kept secret, stands in the middle of the industrial complex which was once the Cellophane production site. It was built as a yeoman's residence in 1500 from blue lias, standing in stark contrast to the red-brick buildings which surround it. The ancient estate of Sydenham, not to be confused with Sydenham Estate as we know it today, predates the house by some 500 years. It once belonged to a Saxon called Chepping, the name Sydenham simply meaning 'wide meadow'. With the Norman conquest of 1066, Chepping lost his lands and the property was given to Roger of Arundel. By 1086 the Domesday Book entry shows that it had tripled in value, describing it as one virgate (a quarter of a hide) with land for one plough with 15 acres.

Roger of Arundel left the property to his son, Robert, who became Robert of Sydenham. For nine generations the estate stayed in the Sydenham family until the death of John Sydenham in 1450. He died with no natural heir and the estate passed to his sister, Joan, who married local man Richard Cave. In 1500, with no male heir, Alice Cave's marriage to Thomas Percival took the property into the ownership of the Percivals. It was as a wedding present that Thomas Percival had the new manor house built, which was the beginnings of the building we see today, albeit expanded and upgraded at various times throughout its history.

The great grandson of Thomas Percival, Richard, was born in 1550. He seems to have been somewhat reckless and married beneath his station. When the marriage failed he left his wife and disappeared to Spain, by which time his father had disowned him.

The south and north faces of Sydenham Manor House.

(FROM THE BRIDGWATER TOWN COUNCIL COLLECTION, COURTESY THE BLAKE MUSEUM)

Four years later Richard, fluent in Spanish, wrote the *Bibliotheca Hispanica*, possibly the first English-Spanish dictionary. On his return to England he found that his wife had already died, having been left in the care of the family of Roger Cave, whose brother-in-law was the Lord Treasurer, and had control of the Navy. Richard Percival found himself a role in his offices.

Meanwhile, out in the English Channel, a Spanish man-of-war had been chased down and the captain had thrown a chest over the side. The English captain, realising that the chest probably contained vital intelligence, recovered it and sailed it to Portsmouth. Papers from the chest, ridden to London and translated by Richard Percival, were found to be plans for the Spanish Armada. As a result, the Spanish had to delay their attempted invasion for a further two years.

The Queen was so delighted with the translation

Richard Percival.

(FROM THE ROGER EVANS COLLECTION)

that Richard Percival was awarded the Duchy of Lancaster and a pension for life. He thus became a hero and his father accepted him back into the home. On his father's death in 1613, Richard sold his inheritance at Sydenham to William Bull and settled in south-west Ireland. William Bull's family were at the manor during the Civil War, when they backed the wrong side, and through the Monmouth Rebellion, when they backed the wrong side again.

The Bull ownership ended in 1700, when Eleanor Bull married George Bubb Dodington. On his death in 1720, the manor passed to his nephew and there then followed five changes of ownership until it was purchased in 1935 by Courtaulds, who wanted to develop a Cellophane plant on the site. Prior to that, however, one of the biggest events ever held in the town took place at the manor – the 1927 Bridgwater Pageant.

CHAPTER 12

Around and About the West Side

Angel Crescent

This was the site of the north gate entrance to the town. The crescent-shaped row of houses was built in 1816 and refurbished in 1986 when the Angel Place shopping precinct was developed.

Binford Place

Running between the bridge and the library, this riverside street was regularly prone to flooding, especially on the spring tides. It was here that the Abbot of Glastonbury paid for the Langport slipway to be built.

In the 1950s the local carnival clubs used this bank for a slippery pole competition. The event began with the various clubs producing their own river-craft by lashing oil drums to tin baths. These were launched, with their crews, from Dunball wharf as the tide rushed in. Paddling frantically, more to stay afloat than for speed, they made their way up to Binford Place, where the race finished. The next

stage of the competition involved the slippery pole, which projected out over the river. With a half crown piece on the far end, the pole was covered in axle grease. I cannot remember anyone actually reaching the coin before falling into the river.

Blake Gardens

Two and a half acres of gardens, alongside the river, form Blake Gardens, unfortunately cut in half when the Blake Bridge and Broadway were opened in 1957. The gardens were purchased by the corporation in 1898 from Mr R.C. Else. The summerhouse and romantic archway, the features of so many old photographs, are long since gone. The bandstand survives and is still used in the summer months for performances.

Blake Street

Named after Robert Blake, who was born there, Blake Street was built around 1500. Purchased by the

Binford Place in flood, c.1954. (COURTESY DOUGLAS ALLEN)

125

Above, right and below: *Views of Blake Gardens c.1905.*
(FROM THE ROGER EVANS COLLECTION)

Bridgwater Imperial Silver Band were regular performers in Blake Gardens, c.1920.
(FROM THE ROGER EVANS COLLECTION)

John Chubb's impression of the Cornhill in earlier days. (FROM THE ROGER EVANS COLLECTION)

borough in 1924, the property became the town's museum. Sedgemoor District Council, to their shame, have considered moving the Blake Museum to the Town Hall as a cost-cutting exercise, having completely lost sight of the heritage value of this sixteenth-century dwelling-place – one of only three buildings to survive from the medieval period, the others being the church and the Old Vicarage.

At the end of Blake Street stands the fourteenth-century mill which used Durleigh Brook for its water-supply and ground corn for the castle. A system of half-round gutters also fed water from here to the town centre. Unfortunately, the interior was gutted by a young arsonist in the 1990s.

Bond Street

Running between Castle Street and Chandos Street, Bond Street was the site of the bonded warehouse when imports and exports formed a major part of local trade.

Castle Street

Built in 1723 by the architect Benjamin Holloway for the Duke of Chandos and then called Chandos Street, this is a superb example of Georgian architecture. At 11 Castle Street is the Bridgwater Arts Centre, which was the first arts centre in Great Britain, set up in 1946. Across the road, most of the buildings, now

largely offices, were taken up by the Mary Stanley Nursing Home, which served as a maternity hospital from 1920 to 1988.

Chandos Street

At the time when Castle Street was called Chandos Street, this was originally called North Back Street.

Clare Street

Once known as Orloue Street, it became Back Street before taking its current name.

The Cornhill

The Cornhill has always been the historic centre of the town. Bridgwater was a market town and the Cornhill's role has already been described in the chapter on fairs and markets. In 1779 an Act was passed to erect a market-house, several houses being demolished to create the necessary space. Before long it became necessary to enlarge it and that work was completed in 1826, when the Cornhill dome was built by a local man called Hutchings. Then, in 1875, 'a handsome and commodious Corn Exchange' was added, and it is that building which we recognise today as the Cornhill. The pineapple on top of the dome is a symbol of welcome rather than an indication of a fruit and vegetable market.

The Cornhill and St Mary's Church. The busy scene would suggest this was Wednesday, market day. c.1904.

(FROM THE ROGER EVANS COLLECTION)

At one time there were railings around the Cornhill, their purpose being to keep livestock and food produce separated. That the railings were removed in 1895 helps to date the multitude of old postcards depicting the Cornhill in latter days. The Cornhill Market was also the last bastion in the country of pounds, shillings and pence. Long after the introduction of decimalisation, Miss Ash, the auctioneer, made the television news when she refused to change. Years after she would still be heard asking, 'Who'll start me with a tanner. Nine pence anybody? A shilling. One and six. Two bob. Half a crown...' The youngsters who had grown up with decimal currency stood by, totally bemused.

The Admiral Blake Statue
This, Bridgwater's best known landmark, amazingly, was not erected until 1900, when public contributions amounting to £1,200 paid for the hollow casting in bronze and the erection of the statue. Originally

The Cornhill, c.1904. All traffic was horse-drawn in those pre-tarmac days.

(FROM THE ROGER EVANS COLLECTION)

Nicholls & Co. at No. 9 The Cornhill, 1865.
(FROM THE BRIDGWATER TOWN COUNCIL COLLECTION,
COURTESY THE BLAKE MUSEUM)

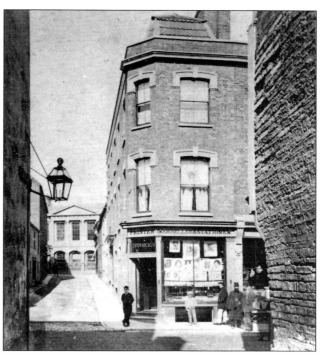

Stokes the stationers at the junction of Fore Street and Court Street, 1865.
(FROM THE BRIDGWATER TOWN COUNCIL COLLECTION,
COURTESY THE BLAKE MUSEUM)

positioned in front of the Cornhill dome, it was controversially moved to its current position at the top end of Fore Street.

The Royal Clarence

For many years, Bridgwater's premier hotel was the Royal Clarence. It was built in 1825 in the Regency style on the site of the former Angel and The Crown. It was originally called the Royal Hotel, until an occasion when the Duke of Clarence, later to become William IV, passed through the town and changed his horses at The Royal. The proprietor sought his majesty's permission to add 'Clarence' in honour of

The Royal Clarence at a time when motors and horses shared the roads. Notice the mattress-like gas container on top of the car.
(FROM THE ROGER EVANS COLLECTION)

A very different looking West India House, c.1865, on Durleigh Road where modern premises have replaced the old thatched inn.

(FROM THE BRIDGWATER TOWN COUNCIL COLLECTION, COURTESY THE BLAKE MUSEUM)

the visit and the rest is history. The plaque on the front of the portico was taken from the old Town Bridge in 1883.

Court Street

Leading from Fore Street to the Court House, this was originally known as Coffee House Lane until 1890, when it took its current title. The Court House is an early-nineteenth-century building of limited architectural interest. However, more significant is

the neighbouring Castle House, the first house anywhere to be built of prefabricated concrete. Built in 1851, its history is dealt with in Chapter 7.

Dampiet Street

Dampiet Street was known originally as Damyate, meaning by the way of the dam, a reference to the dam built to provide the water power for the mill at the bottom of Blake Street. The history of the Unitarian Chapel here is described in Chapter 7.

Looking down Durleigh Road with the Horse and Jockey on the right, c.1865.

(FROM THE BRIDGWATER TOWN COUNCIL COLLECTION, COURTESY THE BLAKE MUSEUM)

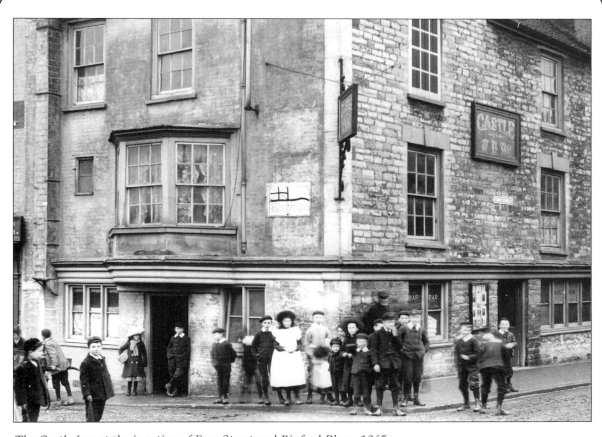

The Castle Inn at the junction of Fore Street and Binford Place, 1865.
(FROM THE BRIDGWATER TOWN COUNCIL COLLECTION, COURTESY THE BLAKE MUSEUM)

Fore Street from the Town Bridge, 1865. Note the serpent-headed chimney on the right, above what is now Thomas Cook's travel agency.

(FROM THE BRIDGWATER TOWN COUNCIL COLLECTION, COURTESY THE BLAKE MUSEUM)

Stokes the stationers, 1865. (FROM THE BRIDGWATER TOWN COUNCIL COLLECTION, COURTESY THE BLAKE MUSEUM)

Hook's the grocers, 1865. (FROM THE BRIDGWATER TOWN COUNCIL COLLECTION, COURTESY THE BLAKE MUSEUM)

Nelson's butchers on the corner of Fore Street, 1902.

(FROM THE BRIDGWATER TOWN COUNCIL COLLECTION, COURTESY THE BLAKE MUSEUM)

Fore Street

Predominantly nineteenth century in style, Fore Street survives from medieval times, when it was known as 'twixt church and bridge'. It is perhaps best to start at the Town Bridge and look up into Fore Street. On our left, in 1865, the Castle Inn dominated this corner. By 1902 Nelson's, the family butcher, traded here and in 1910 it was the premises of London Central. Today it serves as a building society.

Across the road, Nos 2–6 feature an Edwardian façade using attractive terracotta blocks. Particularly interesting are the serpents heads bursting forth from a chimney pot, a feature which can still be seen today.

On the corner of Court Street once stood the premises of Stokes, the stationers and booksellers and it was here that the *Bridgwater Mercury* was produced and where there was a catastrophic fire in 1883.

Next door, at No. 14, were the premises of Hook's, the grocer and provision dealer.

Across the road, on the corner of George Street, once known as Ball's Lane, Archibald Graham ran his stationers and bookshop in 1865. Standing in the doorway are John Ford, Mr Graham and Dr Parsons.

At the top end of Fore Street, Bridgwater could once boast a Marks & Spencer store on the site where, in 1865, Shrimpton & Halson sold ironmongery and to the right of them were the premises of Symons the tailors.

Friarn Street

Friarn Street is the site of the old Grey Friars priory. The Plymouth Brethren, who came to the town in the 1840s, moved from their Gloucester Place premises to Friarn Street in 1868. The street is also the home of

Friarn Street in 1865. On the right is the site of the present postal sorting office.

(FROM THE BRIDGWATER TOWN COUNCIL COLLECTION, COURTESY THE BLAKE MUSEUM)

Archibald Graham, stationer and bookseller, 1865.

(FROM THE BRIDGWATER TOWN COUNCIL COLLECTION, COURTESY BLAKE MUSEUM)

Fore Street in 1865, looking towards the Town Bridge.

(FROM THE BRIDGWATER TOWN COUNCIL COLLECTION, COURTESY BLAKE MUSEUM)

Shrimpton & Halson (above) *were neighbours of Symons the tailors* (below), *1865.*

(BOTH PICTURES FROM THE BRIDGWATER TOWN COUNCIL COLLECTION, COURTESY BLAKE MUSEUM)

Street. Also on the same side is Silver Street, which connects to Little St Mary Street.

The High Street

Once almost twice the width we see it today, there was a row of buildings down the centre of the High Street known as the Cockenrewe, which survived until the early-nineteenth century. After this, the central area served as a taxi rank. Evidence of this remains in the wide pavement area at the front of the Angel Place shopping precinct.

With the development of the precinct, two old pubs disappeared, the Bull and Butcher and the Olde Oake, although their names survive on the brickwork façade. The Galleries night spot was once the Bridgwater Arms and the other night spot, Remedies, was once the Valiant Soldier. An interesting, albeit faded, feature can be seen on the side of the Bridgwater Bookshop, where the faint remains of the words 'W.H. Smith – Saddlery' can just be made out, indicating an earlier use of the premises.

Danger's Ope

This is the narrow lane running between the High Street and the back of St Mary's Church. Ope is archaic for opening, and at one time there was an upstairs room which connected the two rows of shops, forming an arch over this rear entrance to the church.

The Town Hall

The Town Hall, built by C. Knowles using Bridgwater Brick, Wembdon sandstone and Bath

Mrs Alexander's Friarn Street School for Girls, c.1870.
(FROM THE BRIDGWATER TOWN COUNCIL COLLECTION, COURTESY THE BLAKE MUSEUM)

the local Quakers whose Friends' Meeting House was built in 1722 and enlarged in 1801. Running off Friarn Street is Horsepond Lane, once known as Wayhur, which translates as 'horse pond' to which the lane once led.

Running off the other side of Friarn Street is Green Dragon Lane, a narrow alley which runs alongside the Green Dragon Inn leading into Little St Mary

The north side of the High Street, 1890, with the Bull and Butcher (left) *and the Old Oak Inn* (right) *on either side of Beers's cycle store.* (FROM THE BRIDGWATER TOWN COUNCIL COLLECTION, COURTESY THE BLAKE MUSEUM)

The High Street with the central taxi rank, c.1907. (FROM THE ROGER EVANS COLLECTION)

View of the High Street showing the Royal Clarence next to Taylor's Restaurant, c.1906. Note the central taxi rank.

(FROM THE BRIDGWATER TOWN COUNCIL COLLECTION, COURTESY BLAKE MUSEUM)

The south side of the High Street, 1906. (FROM THE ROGER EVANS COLLECTION).

The north side of the High Street with Thompson & Rowe (grocers), Boulting's (glass and china) and the Royal Clarence Hotel, 1865. (FROM THE BRIDGWATER TOWN COUNCIL COLLECTION, COURTESY THE BLAKE MUSEUM)

The White Lion, 1865.   (FROM THE BRIDGWATER TOWN COUNCIL COLLECTION, COURTESY THE BLAKE MUSEUM)

stone for the architectural features, was opened in July 1865. Three storeys high, it is in the Georgian style with a stucco frontage and stands on the site of the old assizes court. For decades now it has hosted the annual carnival concerts, events which bring the greatest number of local residents to its auditorium. On the first floor is the council chamber, now back in use since the re-establishment of a town council for the parish. In the Charter Hall is an old photograph showing how the main hall was used during the riots linked with the brickyard strike, when it housed the troops and police involved in that episode.

Lamb Lane
Lamb Lane is the short lane which runs alongside The Duke, formerly the Duke of Monmouth and originally the Lamb Inn.

Mansion House Inn and Lane
The Mansion House Inn dates back to at least 1537, when it was described as a church house being conveyed to two leading townsmen. It was occasionally used as an entertainment centre and in 1722 the top floor was used as the local grammar school. In all probability, the top floor would at one time have been a large meeting room, or assembly room, hence the 'Mansion House' title. In 1765 the corporation arranged the demolition and rebuilding of the premises which resulted in the school moving elsewhere, although by 1788 it had moved back. In 1799 a soup kitchen was established here, by which time at

Mansion House Lane with the Shipwright's Arms on the left and the Mansion House Inn, 1865.

(FROM THE ROGER EVANS COLLECTION).

139

The buildings where the Angel Place shopping precinct now stands included a candle factory and a tea warehouse. The gable-ended building is the Bull and Butcher Inn.
(FROM THE BRIDGWATER TOWN COUNCIL COLLECTION, COURTESY THE BLAKE MUSEUM)

least part of the premises had already been an inn for many years. The short lane which runs alongside the Mansion House is Mansion House Lane.

Old Oak Lane

Running parallel with Mansion House Lane, between the Angel Place precinct and Barclays Bank, is an alleyway known as Old Oak Lane, reflecting its position alongside the former Old Oak Inn.

King Square

King Square once formed a significant part of the old castle site. The fine houses on the south and west

Old Oak Lane, c.1904.   (FROM THE ROGER EVANS COLLECTION)

Bridgwater Cycling Club outside the Bristol Arms Commercial Hotel, 1865.
(FROM THE BRIDGWATER TOWN COUNCIL COLLECTION, COURTESY THE BLAKE MUSEUM)

The east side of King Square, 1865. Note the crushed stone road with bricked walkway.
(FROM THE BRIDGWATER TOWN COUNCIL COLLECTION, COURTESY THE BLAKE MUSEUM)

sides of the square date back to the 1820s and the new council offices on the north side have been sympathetically designed to blend with the earlier buildings. Also on the north side, the Masonic Lodge, built in 1912, features narrow slits through which lodge members could spy strangers waiting to enter.

The centrepiece of the square is the war memorial, erected in 1924 and unveiled by Lord Cavan. It features a statue of a mother and child, representing civilisation. Beneath the mother's feet are figures representing strife, bloodshed, corruption and despair. In one hand she holds a globe of the world and in the other the Book of Law.

King Street

On the corner of King Street and Dampiet Street is the old Wesleyan Chapel, built in 1816, with columned porticoes. The King Street Methodist Chapel was a follow-up to that already established in Monmouth Street. The King Street premises closed around 1970 and became a furniture store. At the time of writing they are being redeveloped.

Northgate

The original Northgate was an arched entrance to the town at the junction of Angel Crescent and the

North Street in flood in 1899, showing the old Malt Shovel Inn at the far end.
(FROM THE BRIDGWATER TOWN COUNCIL COLLECTION, COURTESY THE BLAKE MUSEUM)

North Street, 1865.
(FROM THE BRIDGWATER TOWN COUNCIL COLLECTION, COURTESY THE BLAKE MUSEUM)

The newly built Malt Shovel Inn, 1905. (FROM THE BRIDGWATER TOWN COUNCIL COLLECTION, COURTESY THE BLAKE MUSEUM)

present-day Northgate. Starkey, Knight & Ford once had a brewery here, closed in the 1950s, on the site of the present-day Sedgemoor Splash swimming pool. The field behind still bears the name 'the Brewery Field'.

North Street

One of the oldest streets in the town, North Street was the last stretch of houses on the north side, with dwellings as far as the Malt Shovel Inn but nothing beyond that until after 1840. One of the older inns in the town, the present-day Annie's Bar, was once known as the North Pole Inn and the house next door The Igloo.

The Malt Shovel Inn
The original Malt Shovel Inn was demolished in 1904 and replaced by the inn we see today.

Penel Orlieu

Bridgwater's most unusual place name, Penel Orlieu is derived from the junction of Orloue Street (later to be called Prickett's Lane and now Market Street) and Paynell Street (now Clare Street). Until 1935 this was the centre of the cattle market and was the area where cattle and pigs were sold, sheep being dealt with in West Street. Where the cinema now stands, along with the car park across the road, is the area where the market was held. This was also the site of the

The White Horse Inn at Penel Orlieu, 1865, with the Roundhouse in the background.

(FROM THE BRIDGWATER TOWN COUNCIL COLLECTION, COURTESY THE BLAKE MUSEUM)

142

Penel Orlieu cattle market, 1907.   (FROM THE ROGER EVANS COLLECTION)

Penel Orlieu, overcrowded during the cattle sales, c.1910.   (FROM THE ROGER EVANS COLLECTION)

The Three Tuns Inn in Penel Orlieu, c.1880.

Three Tuns Inn, which was demolished to make way for the market.

Across the road, between the Blake Arms and the Roundhouse, once stood the White Horse Inn. A few older residents of the town still refer to this area as Pea Cross, reflecting the market cross which once stood here. The cross was demolished in 1769 and replaced with St Mary's Cross from the churchyard. This in turn was demolished in 1830. Within living memory there was also a watering trough in the centre of Penel Orlieu.

The photographs on page 143 show how over-crowded the Penel Orlieu area became on market day. The whole road was blocked, despite this being

Looking into Penel Orlieu from West Street. North Street goes off to the left. The gates of the cattle market can just be made out down the street on the left. Note the two police officers posing for the camera.

St Mary's Church – note the railings, installed to keep cattle away from the yew tree.

(FROM THE ROGER EVANS COLLECTION)

the only way through the town for those travelling on the A39.

The Odeon Cinema
Due to the number of times these premises change ownership, I shall refer to the town's one surviving cinema by its original name – The Odeon. It opened

in 1936 when the Argyle and Sutherland Pipe Band paraded through the town at the grand opening. So many people turned up for the occasion that traffic came to a standstill. The building once boasted an ornamental roof supported on columns. The columns survive but the roof has long since gone, detracting from the balance of the building. In recent years the cinema has been known both as The Classic and, at the time of writing, Scott Cinemas.

The Palace Theatre and Night Club
The Palace Theatre was officially opened in March 1916, when it was known as The Empire, with a seating capacity of 600. The first production staged there was *A Pair of Silk Stockings*. In 1938 the premises were closed due to lack of safety precautions and, when it reopened in 1940, it was to entertain the troops, providing ENSA entertainment during the war years. It reopened as a cinema in 1950 and remained as such until August 1985. It seemed then that it may never be reopened and, over the years of its closure, became an eyesore, especially for those entering the town from the Minehead direction. Fortunately for the image of the town, the brothers Bob and Clive Lilley saw the potential to develop it once again as an entertainment centre, this time as a nightclub. Within months the frontage of the building was restored to its former splendour and the Lilley brothers were presented with a well-deserved 'Environmental Enhancement' award by the Bridgwater and District Civic Society.

West Bow Corner
On the corner of West Street and Penel Orlieu was West Bow House, the demolition of which, begun in August 1901, is shown in the photograph below.

West Bow Corner.

(FROM THE ROGER EVANS COLLECTION)

The exposed wattle and daub wall of the Old Vicarage Restaurant.   (FROM THE ROGER EVANS COLLECTION)

St Mary Street

Being on the main road out of the town, it is no surprise that there were several inns and coaching houses along St Mary Street. The Rose and Crown dates back to the fourteenth century, the Tudor Restaurant, which is not Tudor, dates from around 1600 and the Waterloo Inn is early-eighteenth century. The Three Crowns, which closed a few years ago, had a skittle alley along the walls of which were iron rings, once used to tie up the horses stabled there. The Baptist Chapel was built in 1837. St Saviour's Avenue, which runs off St Mary Street, is late-nineteenth-century and marks the approximate site of St Saviours Church, which stood just outside the south gate from 1530 to at least 1703.

Bridgwater Docks with the Chandos glass kiln clearly visible in the background.   (FROM THE ROGER EVANS COLLECTION)

The Emma, *owned by David Nurse and Ben Pearce, moored up on the West Quay.*   (From the Roger Evans Collection)

The Old Vicarage

St Mary Street contains a row of fourteenth-century cottages which includes the Old Vicarage Restaurant, given in the sixteenth century by Edward de Chedzoy to be used as a vicarage, which is how it remained until around 100 years ago. The original building was of wattle and daub construction, and a glass-covered example of this is exposed in the archway which leads to the back of the premises. On the front wall is an unusual opening which appears to be bottle shaped. One theory is that it was used to pass tankards of mulled drinks out to the coachmen, who remained aboard their stagecoaches as their passengers dined inside in the warm.

The Old Vicarage is certainly the oldest domestic premises in the town, only the church itself dating back any further. As a one-time coaching house, it continued life as Steynings Tea Rooms before reverting to its Old Vicarage title.

Marycourt

Marycourt, now the Carnival Inn, was a much more interesting building in its former life. It has also been known as Judge Jeffreys House, which is a misnomer as Jeffreys never came to Bridgwater. It was Colonel Percy Kirke, who came in advance of the Bloody Assizes, who stayed here (see Chapter 4). It was whilst softening up rebels captured after the Monmouth Rebellion that he ordered the execution of anyone who pleaded their innocence, ordering them to be hung, drawn and quartered on the Cornhill, from the market cross. It is alleged that a young Bridgwater girl, whose lover was due to be hanged, went to Kirke and pleaded for her lover's life to be spared. She had nothing to offer in return other than herself. Kirke accepted her offer and that night slept with her in Marycourt. As dawn broke, she reminded him of their bargain – that in return for her favours, he would return her lover to her keeping. Kirke drew back the curtains and pointed to the Cornhill, declaring she could take her lover as promised. He had already been hanged from the market cross.

The Bijou and Imperial Cinemas

Long since disappeared, the Bijou cinema was the first in the town, opening in October 1910 at No. 25 St Mary Street. Just 23 days later the Imperial Cinema opened at the other end of St Mary Street where it joins with Green Dragon Lane. It survived just two months and then reopened, was rebuilt and closed again in 1912.

Valetta Place

Named after the capital of Malta, this row of houses was built for sea captains in the mid-nineteenth century, when shipping was at its peak. For many

The Lavinia *moored at the West Quay.*
(FROM THE ROGER EVANS COLLECTION)

years, the house at the river end of the terrace was the home of a basket weaver.

Close to the other end of Valetta Place are the remains of the Chandos Glass Kiln. Originally 75ft high, it was a failed attempt by the Duke of Chandos to create a glass industry in the town. Still intact in 1942, it was demolished to provide hardcore for the runway extensions at Westonzoyland aerodrome. The stump of the kiln is now a listed building!

West Quay

West Quay, in my opinion, is grossly underrated. There is a character to it which is best viewed at a distance from across the river. The buildings now known as Fisherman's Wharf were once the site of the Oddfellows Hall, where one of Bridgwater's first cinemas, the Electric Theatre, opened in 1913. Within three weeks the *Mercury* had put the kiss of death on the venture by declaring it to be 'getting more

Gardner's Dining Rooms, on the corner of West Street and North Street, 1902. They were always busy on market day. (FROM THE BRIDGWATER TOWN COUNCIL COLLECTION, COURTESY THE BLAKE MUSEUM)

successful every week'. The following week it closed, never to reopen.

West Street

West Street, thanks to the abundance of underground wells, was densely populated by terraced cottages and courtyards. These were demolished as part of a slum clearance scheme, totally changing the character of the street.

Wednesday morning market day in West Street.
(FROM THE BRIDGWATER TOWN COUNCIL COLLECTION, COURTESY THE BLAKE MUSEUM)

CHAPTER 13

Did You Know?

Bridgwater Bowling Club, May 1909.

(FROM THE ROGER EVANS COLLECTION)

In 1487, Henry VIII declared Bridgwater to be a county in its own right.

In 1785, Bridgwater was the first town to petition Parliament for the abolition of slavery.

Bridgwater-born Frances Barkley (1769–1845) was the first woman to circumnavigate the world twice. She was also the first European woman to set foot in Hawaii, British Columbia and Vietnam.

Captain George Lewis Browne (1784–1856) was a member of the Unitarian Chapel in Dampiet Street and is now buried in the old Wembdon Road cemetery. He fought alongside Nelson on the *Victory* at the Battle of Trafalgar and was present at his funeral. Another Bridgwater man, William Hubber, a sailor, died at his home in Monmouth Street on 7 November 1859, aged 103. At the time of his death, he was in receipt of poor relief, but in his prime he was another Bridgwater man who fought at the Battle of Trafalgar.

Denis Heron (1829–1895) who lived in Salmon Parade and is buried in the Bristol Road Cemetery, fought in the Crimea at the Charge of the Light Brigade.

Victoria Road was originally known as Malt Shovel Lane and Victoria Park as Malt Shovel Park.

The first motorised town taxi service was launched by the Bridgwater Motor Co. in 1909.

Bridgwater once had four cinemas operating at the same time (1920s); the Odeon and the Palace in Penel Orlieu, the Arcade in Eastover (later known as the Rex) and a regular cinema in the Town Hall.

The first time that anyone as young as 18 was allowed to vote was at a Bridgwater by-election in1970 when Tom King was elected for the first time.

Annie's Bar was once known as the North Pole Inn and the house next door was called the Igloo.

Outside the Bridgwater Motor Co., c.1910.

CHAPTER 14

Bridgwater Snapshots

Celebrity Visitors

Samuel Taylor Coleridge was a frequent visitor to Bridgwater and preached on at least two occasions at the Unitarian Chapel. He would walk all the way from Nether Stowey, preach in Bridgwater and then walk to Taunton to repeat his performance there.
(FROM THE ROGER EVANS COLLECTION)

Princess Alexandra opening the new open-air Bridgwater Lido in 1960. Wearing the mayoral chains is Alderman E.J. (Jack) Davies and to his right is George Poskitt.

(COURTESY DOUGLAS ALLEN)

Princess Diana on her visit to Bridgwater in April 1991.
(COURTESY KEITH PAINTER)

Maritime Past and Present

Remnants of a maritime past still line the quaysides at Bridgwater Docks.
(FROM THE ROGER EVANS COLLECTION)

The Bridgwater and District Civic Society continue to play their part in preserving the town's heritage. The ruined navigation buoy (above) was restored as a Society project and this picture (right) completes the before and after comparison. The Society has also been responsible for the return of the Town Bridge lanterns and the restoration of the crane on the West Quay.
(FROM THE ROGER EVANS COLLECTION)

The redevelopment of the docks into a marina has attracted an ever-growing flotilla of barges and river craft to the former docks.
(FROM THE ROGER EVANS COLLECTION)

The Spirit of Bridgwater

In 2005, as a companion to the statue of Admiral Blake, the Spirit of Carnival was unveiled to commemorate the 400th anniversary of the Gunpowder Plot, which Bridgwater celebrates with its annual spectacular carnival.

(FROM THE ROGER EVANS COLLECTION)

These postcards, dating from around 1910, reflect the local sense of humour.

(FROM THE ROGER EVANS COLLECTION)

Appendix
Early Members of Parliament for Bridgwater

1295	John of the Weye	Walter Jacob
1298	John of Sydenham	William Jacob
1300	Richard of Roborough	Adam the Palmer
1301	William the Large	Jordan the Parmenter
1302	Walter King	Richard Dygoun
1305	John Savan	Richard of Roborough
1306	Richard the Wylde	John of Savan
1307	Richard the Wylde	Lawrence Grey
	John Savan	John of the Weye
1309	Richard Woodcock	William the Gardiner
1311	John of Cloteworthy	Stephen of Toukerton
	Richard Woodcock	Walter the Chepman
1312	Richard Woodcock	Ralph atte Wood
1313	Richard of Stiklepath	Roger Broun
	Wm Forthred	Ralph atte Wood
	Richard of Stiklepath	Ralph atte Wood
1314	Ralph Pope	Walter Fychet
1315	Thomas Rogeroun	Walter of Watchet
1319	John Bennet	Walter Purchas
1321	Adam de Leghe	John of Dunster
1322	John of Forde	Wm. Rogeron
	Adam of Leghe	David the Palmer
1324	Walter of Enmore	John of Coumbe
1325	John of Ilebruere	John Saladyn
1326-7	Thomas Boye	Roger Person
1328	Hugh Celerer	Adam of Portland
1328-9	John the Warener	Richard the Dyer
1330	David the Palmer	Thomas Boye
1332	Walter of Enmore	John Eveson
	Richard Coleford	John Cronill
1334	John Cronnill	Adam of Legh
	Thomas Eremyte	Walter of Eston
1335	Richard of Coker	Adam of Legh
1336	John of Somerton	John of Hungerford
	William Duncan	William Syward
1337	Thomas Boye	Walter of Eston
1338	Jan Saladyn	William Boye
	John Saladyn	John of Petherton
1340	Henry the Bakelere	Simon the Nywecombe
	Robert Wake	John Saladyn
1341	John the Hare	John of Lenge
1344	Richard Boye	Gilbert the Large
1346	Edward Babbe	John Boye
1348	Robert Wake	William Topet
1351	Roger atte Crosse	Walter Don
1352	Thomas Large	William of Welde
1354	Robert of Plympton	Thomas Large
1355	Thomas Large	William Crych
1358	Adam Beste	Nicholas Boye
1360	John Bokland	John Gelhampton

1361	John Wyard	Richard Shapwick
1362	William Crych	Robert Plympton
1363	William Crych	John Smok
1366	Robert Plympton	William Crych
1368	William Crych	Thomas Engilby
1369	John Lof	Adam Leybourne
1371	Adam Beste	William Tannere
1372	Adam Beste	Hugh Mareys
1373	Walter Taillour	Adam Westleghe
1377	John Palmer	William Blacche
	William Thomere	John Sydenham
1378	John Palmer	John Sydenham
1380	John Fytelton	William THomer
1381	John Loof	John Henton
1383	John Palmer	Humphrey Plomer
	John Palmer	William Thomere
1384	John Palmer	John Wynde
	John Loof	Thomas Wyke
1385	William Thomere	John Palmer
1386	John Sydenham	Richard Mayne
1388	John Sydenham	Richard Mayne
	John Palmer	John Wynde
1390	John Palmer	William Thomere
1391	William Thomere	John Sydenham
1393	William Thomere	Robert Bosom
1394	John Palmer	John Cole
1395, 1397	William Thomere	John Kedwelly
1397, 1402	William Thomere	John Kedwelly
1406	William Thomere	William Gascoign
1407	William Gascoign	Richard Warde
1410	William Gascoign	John Kedwelly
1413	William Gascoign	William Gosse
1414, 1417	William Gascoign	Thomas Cave
1419	William Gascoign	Richard Mayn
1420	William Gascoign	Martin Jacob
1421	William Gascoign	James Fitz-James
1422	William Gascoign	John Gonne
1423	John Pyt	Martin Jacob
1425	William Gascoign	John Gonne or John Pytte
1425	John Pytte	Thomas Cave
1427, 1429	William Gascoign	John Pytte
1431	Alexander Hody	Edward Coleford
1432	John Pytte	Thomas Cave
1433	Alexander Hody	Robert Halswell
1435	John Pytte	David Baker
1437	John Gonne	Geoffrey Mone
1442	William Dodesham	William Andrew
1447	Robert Cotys	Thomas Burgoyne
1449	John Maunsel junr	William Gosse
	Reginald Sowdeley	Thomas Dryyfelld
1450	John Hille	William Howell
1453	John Maunsel junr	William Warde
1455	Thomas Lewkenore	William Plusshe
1460	William Gosse	John Croppe
1467	John Kendale	James Fitz-James
1472	Sir Thomas Tremayle	
1483	William Hody	John Hymerford

Bibliography

Baumber, Michael, General-at-Sea (1989), *Robert Blake*, John Murray, London

Belshaw, Guy (2004), *Bridgwater St Matthew's Fair: An Illustrated History*, Telford, New Era Publications

Cheshunt, Bill (1998), *Legend of the Little Liberty Bell*, Bridgeton Antiquarian League, Bridgeton, New Jersey

Clarkson, Thomas (1807), *The History of the Rise, Progress and Accomplishment of the Abolition of the African Slave-Trade by the British Parliament*, L. Taylor, London

Dilks, T.B. (ed.) (1933), *Bridgwater Borough Archives 1200–1377*, Somerset Record Society, Taunton

Dunning, R.W. (ed.) (1992), *The Victoria History of the County of Somerset Vol. VI: Bridgwater and Neighbouring Parishes*, Oxford University Press Oxford

Evans, Roger, (1994), *Bridgwater With and Without the 'e'*, Roger Evans, Bridgwater

Evans, Roger (2000), *Forgotten Heroes of Bridgwater*, Roger Evans, Bridgwater

Evans, Roger (2004), *Somerset's Forgotten Heroes*, Dovecote Press, Wimborne

Hawkins, Mac (1988), *Somerset at War*, Dovecote Press, Wimborne

Jarman, S.G. (1889), *History of Bridgwater*, Elliot Stock, London

Murless, Brian J. (1989), *Bridgwater Docks and the River Parrett*, Somerset County Council, Taunton

Powell, Revd A.H. (1907), *The Ancient Borough of Bridgwater*, Page & Son, Bridgwater

Raven, John J. (1906), *The Bells of England*, Methuen, London

Williams, D. (1997), *Bridgwater Inns Past and Present*, Abbey Press, Crewkerne

Acknowledgement for illustrations

The photographs from the Bridgwater Town Council Collection, now in the care of the Blake Museum, are predominantly the work of Robert Gillo.

Subscribers

Kevin P. Abbott, Bridgwater, Somerset

Mrs Phyllis Doreen Allen, Bridgwater, Somerset

David Roy Ashman, Bridgwater, Somerset

Samuel George Earl Baker, Valetta Place, Bridgwater

Linda and Martin Barnes, Minehead

G.R.J.H. Beale, Clarendon House, Bridgwater, Somerset

Harry Bell, Bridgwater, Somerset

Alan W.H. Biddiscombe

W.H. (Bill) May Biffen, Retired Funeral Director, Bridgwater, Somerset

Mr Paul B. Billing, Cannington, Somerset

Bridgwater – La Ciotat Link Society

Mr Alfred J. Britton, Bridgwater, Somerset

Peter K. Broxholme, Westonzoyland, Somerset

John and Ruth Capell

Malcolm L. Carr, Bridgwater, Somerset

Mr Desmond J. Carver, Saltlands, Bridgwater, Somerset

Valerie D. Chilcott, Bridgwater, Somerset

Malcolm Chorley, Bridgwater, Somerset

Gordon and Sylvia Churchyard, Pawlett

Miss P. Clark, King George Avenue, Bridgwater

David W. Cooze, Bridgwater, Somerset

Marion J. Cotton, Bridgwater, Somerset

Kathleen M. Cowles, Othery, Somerset

The Crossman Family, Bridgwater

A. Curran, Chilton Trinity, Bridgwater, Somerset

Geoff and Tricia Date, now of Totnes

June Datson, Weston-Super-Mare

Elsie May Day, Bridgwater, Somerset

John M. Day

Wilfred Sydney Dennison, Bridgwater, Somerset

Jan Derewicz, Upminster

Joanne Draper, Bridgwater, Somerset

Mr Phillip Dyer P.A., Burnham-on-Sea, Somerset

Ruth Fargnioli, Cannington

Teresa L. Ford, West Street, Bridgwater

Clifford J. Frost, Bridgwater, Somerset

Christina Gardener-White

P.D. Gazzard, Othery, Somerset

Doreen L. Gibbs

Mr and Mrs Keith Giles, Bridgwater, Somerset

Paul and Emma Gover, Watergate Hotel, Bridgwater

Lorraine Grief, Torrington, North Devon

Graham A. Gunningham, Bridgwater, Somerset

Ron Hawkes, Cannington, Somerset

Rodney L.J. Hawkins, Bridgwater, Somerset

Antony J. Higgs, Ontario, Canada

Harold W. Hill, Bridgwater, Somerset

Mike and Rosalind Holman, Bridgwater

Kieron B. Howes, Bridgwater, Somerset

Ronald A. Hubbard, Bridgwater, Somerset

Betty M. Innalls (née Crocker), Bridgwater, Somerset

Derek Irish, Bridgwater, Somerset

Norman Ives, Bridgwater, Somerset

Rod C. Jenkins, Cannington, Bridgwater

Robin S. Jennings, Bridgwater, Somerset

Pam Kable, Bridgwater, Somerset

John Kearle, North Petherton, Bridgwater

Jacqueline J. Kelly, Bridgwater, Somerset

Mark Kerslake (deceased), and Steven Webber, Wembdon, Bridgwater

George J. Lakeman, Bridgwater, Somerset

Mr Derek J. and Mrs Mary R. Lawley, Bridgwater, Somerset

J. Lomen, Bridgwater, Somerset

Mr Barrie Lovell, Bridgwater, Somerset

Sue Manley, Bridgwater, Somerset

Paul and Lorraine Mansfield, Cardiff

Mr Michael A. Mardon, Bridgwater, Somerset

Mr and Mrs Miles, Woolavington, Somerset

Mr Michael John Morgan, Bridgwater, Somerset

Peter, Suzanna and Richard Nurse, Cannington

Graham J. Palmer, Bridgwater, Somerset

Ken Parker, Bridgwater, Somerset

Wenda J. Passmore, Broomfield, Somerset

Roger Perren, Bridgwater, Somerset

Michael J. Perry

Mr Ivor M. Peters

Eric S. Pike, North Petherton

W.J. Pitman

Kevin Pollard, Bridgwater, Somerset

Mr and Mrs D. Poole, Bridgwater, Somerset

The Popham Family, Bridgwater, Somerset

Robert Pudner, Bridgwater Library

Ann Redman, Bridgwater

Mr and Mrs S. Regan, Durleigh, Somerset

Rick and Wendy Remiszewski, Bridgwater, Somerset

Ken and Heather Richards, Bridgwater, Somerset

Den and Jean Rossiter, Bridgwater

Mike Searle, Bridgwater, Somerset

Raymond Searle, Bridgwater, Somerset

Jeff Slocombe, Bridgwater, Somerset

Barrie W.C. Smith, Bridgwater

Mr and Mrs F.W. Smith, Bridgwater, Somerset

Ron and Gill Smith, Chilton Polden, Bridgwater

Mr David John Speed, Bridgwater, Somerset

David H. Stanley

Helen L. Stepney, Bridgwater, Somerset

Paul M. Stokes, Chilton Trinity, Somerset

Angela Tarr, Bridgwater, Somerset

Miss Elizabeth D. Terry, Bridgwater, Somerset

Craig I. Thomas, Bridgwater, Somerset

Esme Thompson, Spetisbury, Dorset

Neil and Beth Thompson, Woolavington

Mr Dennis J.E.F. Turner, Bridgwater, Somerset

Ralph Venning, (B.R. Lorry Driver), Bridgwater, Somerset

Ian J. Walker J.P., Bridgwater, Somerset

John F.W. Walling, Newton Abbot, Devon

Glynn W. Watson, Enfield, Middlesex

S.L. and M.J. Wey, Bridgwater, Somerset

Colin Woodland, Crediton, Devon

Pamela M.B. Woodland

Tony Woodland, Bridgwater, Somerset

Sandra Woodland, Penygraig, South Wales

Community Histories Further Reading

The Book of Addiscombe • Canning and Clyde Road
Residents Association and Friends
The Book of Addiscombe, Vol. II • Canning and Clyde Road
Residents Association and Friends
The Book of Ashburton • Stuart Hands and Pete Webb
The Book of Axminster with Kilmington •
Les Berry and Gerald Gosling
* The Book of Axmouth & the Undercliff •
Ted Gosling and Mike Clement
The Book of Bakewell • Trevor Brighton
The Book of Bampton • Caroline Seward
The Book of Barnstaple • Avril Stone
The Book of Barnstaple, Vol. II • Avril Stone
The Book of The Bedwyns • Bedwyn History Society
* Bere Regis Past and Present • Rodney Legg and
John Pitfield
The Book of Bergh Apton • Geoffrey I. Kelly
The Book of Bickington • Stuart Hands
The Book of Bideford • Peter Christie and Alison Grant
Blandford Forum: A Millennium Portrait •
Blandford Forum Town Council
* The Book of Blofield • Barbara Pilch
The Book of Boscastle • Rod and Anne Knight
The Book of Bourton-on-the-Hill, Batsford and
Sezincote • Allen Firth
The Book of Bramford • Bramford
Local History Group
The Book of Breage & Germoe • Stephen Polglase
The Book of Bridestowe • D. Richard Cann
* The Book of Bridgwater • Roger Evans
The Book of Bridport • Rodney Legg
The Book of Brixham • Frank Pearce
The Book of Buckfastleigh • Sandra Coleman
The Book of Buckland Monachorum & Yelverton • Pauline
Hamilton-Leggett
The Book of Budleigh Salterton • D. Richard Cann
The Book of Carharrack • Carharrack Old
Cornwall Society
The Book of Carshalton • Stella Wilks and Gordon
Rookledge
The Parish Book of Cerne Abbas • Vivian and
Patricia Vale
The Book of Chagford • Iain Rice
The Book of Chapel-en-le-Frith • Mike Smith
The Book of Chittlehamholt with
Warkleigh & Satterleigh • Richard Lethbridge
The Book of Chittlehampton • Various
The Book of Codford • Romy Wyeth
The Book of Colney Heath • Bryan Lilley
The Book of Constantine • Moore and Trethowan
The Book of Cornwood and Lutton • Compiled by
the People of the Parish
The Book of Crediton • John Heal
The Book of Creech St Michael • June Small

The Book of Crowcombe, Bicknoller and
Sampford Brett • Maurice and Joyce Chidgey
The Book of Crudwell • Tony Pain
The Book of Cullompton • Compiled by the
People of the Parish
The Book of Dawlish • Frank Pearce
The Book of Dulverton, Brushford,
Bury & Exebridge • Dulverton and District
Civic Society
The Book of Dunster • Hilary Binding
The Book of Easton • Easton Village History Project
The Book of Edale • Gordon Miller
The Ellacombe Book • Sydney R. Langmead
* The Book of Elmsett • Elmsett Local History Group
The Book of Exmouth • W.H. Pascoe
* The Book of Fareham • Lesley Burton and
Brian Musselwhite
The Book of Grampound with Creed • Bane and Oliver
The Book of Gosport • Lesley Burton and
Brian Musselwhite
The Book of Haughley • Howard Stephens
The Book of Hayle • Harry Pascoe
The Book of Hayling Island & Langstone • Peter Rogers
The Book of Helston • Jenkin with Carter
The Book of Hemyock • Clist and Dracott
The Book of Herne Hill • Patricia Jenkyns
The Book of Hethersett • Hethersett Society
Research Group
The Book of High Bickington • Avril Stone
The Book of Honiton • Gerald Gosling
The Book of Ilsington • Dick Wills
* The Book of Kessingland • Maureen and Eric Long
The Book of Kingskerswell • Carsewella Local
History Group
The Book of Lamerton • Ann Cole and Friends
Lanner, A Cornish Mining Parish • Sharron
Schwartz and Roger Parker
The Book of Leigh & Bransford • Malcolm Scott
The Second Book of Leigh & Bransford • Malcolm Scott
The Book of Litcham with Lexham & Mileham • Litcham
Historical and Amenity Society
The Book of Loddiswell • Loddiswell Parish
History Group
The New Book of Lostwithiel • Barbara Fraser
The Book of Lulworth • Rodney Legg
The Book of Lustleigh • Joe Crowdy
The Book of Lydford • Compiled by Barbara Weeks
The Book of Lyme Regis • Rodney Legg
The Book of Manaton • Compiled by the
Peopleof the Parish
The Book of Markyate • Markyate Local History Society
The Book of Mawnan • Mawnan Local History Group
The Book of Meavy • Pauline Hemery
The Book of Mere • Dr David Longbourne

For details of any of the above titles or if you are
interested in writing your own history, please
contact: Commissioning Editor, Community
Histories, Halsgrove House, Lower Moor Way,
Tiverton, Devon EX16 6SS, England; email:
katyc@halsgrove.com

* *2006 publications*